BUILDING
PUBLIC
TRUST

BUILDING
PUBLIC
TRUST

The Future of Corporate Reporting

Samuel A. DiPiazza Jr.
CEO, PricewaterhouseCoopers

Robert G. Eccles
President, Advisory Capital Partners

JOHN WILEY & SONS, INC.

ISBN 0-471-26151-3
ISBN 0-471-27134-9 (SP–19,000)
ISBN 0-471-28169-7 (SP–1,000)

Printed in the United States of America.

10 9 8 7 6 5 4 3 2 1

Foreword

For the financial services community, this is a time of important change. New technologies, especially the Internet and broadband, continue to change how we do almost everything from making markets and conducting research to reporting corporate results. Ease of access and the broad availability of financial information have brought millions of new investors into the market. But since the closing months of 2001, these enormously positive trends have been paralleled by a loud, almost universal cry for reform in how and what companies report to the capital markets, and in the disciplines and processes that underlie corporate reporting—accounting, auditing, governance, and regulation. Can the revolution in technology be the great enabler of these reforms as well?

The strongest cries for reform have come from the United States in the wake of the largest bankruptcy in that country's history, the abrupt and unanticipated failure of Enron. The cries for reform have continued, as Andersen, one of the world's great accounting and auditing firms, has been rent asunder. But the kinds of behavior that have elicited the outcry are not limited to the United States. The problem and the challenge are global.

Because the investing public is now so large, and because employees in public companies are more aware than ever that their careers depend on the success of their companies, what might in decades past have been a crisis behind closed doors often becomes a matter of the broadest public concern. Corporate reporting is an intricate discipline, but everyone from the executive suite and corporate boardroom to the storefront brokerage firm understands its importance to themselves, to their companies, and to their countries.

It is my contention that the future of corporate reporting depends on the crafting and adoption of new concepts and practices better fitted to today's technology. The future of reporting depends *no less* on the development and adoption of new technologies than on the new concepts and practices to which many people are looking for solutions to the present crisis.

Today's capital markets are at the leading edge of complex information technology. But some things are simple and always will be simple. The effectiveness of the world's capital markets depends on public trust, and trust depends on the timely availability of complete, relevant, and reliable information—in a word, it depends on appropriate levels of *transparency.*

Ultimate responsibility for ensuring that shareholders and other stakeholders receive the information they require lies with corporate executives and their boards. Responsibility also lies with the public accounting profession, which periodically updates accounting and reporting guidelines in cooperation with regulatory authorities, and bears responsibility for applying those guidelines with objectivity and impartiality. Investors and others who use the information also bear responsibility for using it conscientiously in assessing corporate performance and making investment decisions.

There is an urgent need for all participants in the capital markets, from investors and analysts to CEOs and regulators, to rededicate themselves to transparent corporate reporting. For this reason, I am delighted to introduce this new book co-authored by Sam DiPiazza, chief executive officer of PricewaterhouseCoopers, and Bob Eccles, formerly a professor at Harvard Business School. Pointing the way toward necessary solutions, this book enables the debate. It is well reasoned and fair. It highlights a range of needs from old-fashioned personal responsibility to powerful new financial reporting technologies like Extensible Business Reporting Language (XBRL).

I have every confidence that out of recent disappointments and ordeals there will emerge the revised, much more robust corporate reporting framework demanded by the world's financial markets. But even the best framework requires participants of integrity to deliver its potential. The future belongs to men and women—in all parts of the world—who can realize that potential through the brilliance of their innovations and their adherence to professional integrity.

WICK SIMMONS
Chairman and Chief Executive Officer
The Nasdaq Stock Market, Inc.

Preface

S ome will ask, "Why have you written this book?" Our own question is different: "How could we *not* have written this book?" There is a time to stand up and be counted—to stand up and offer one's best. Hence this book, addressing a topic that has been forcibly brought to the world's attention: the future of corporate reporting in a time when major business failures and a stiff critique of the practices of auditors and influential securities analysts have shaken the public trust.

The epicenter of this earthquake has been in the United States, focused particularly on the Enron bankruptcy and the conduct of Enron's independent auditor, Andersen. However, the global capital markets are so closely integrated that aftershocks have been felt around the world.

Crisis is opportunity. Virtually every participant in what we have called the Corporate Reporting Supply Chain is looking for new answers, new ways to assure investors and other stakeholders that the information they are receiving enables them to understand companies in detail and in depth. We hope that this book stimulates dialogue among all of us who are responsible for building public trust in the markets, on which the progress of society in all parts of the world depends.

Samuel A. DiPiazza Jr.
Robert G. Eccles

Subject Matter Experts

Every link in what this book calls the Corporate Reporting Supply Chain is a topic in itself, to which experts are devoting their careers. We could not have hoped to write about each link, let alone propose improvements and fundamentally new reforms, without the help of a network of outstanding subject matter experts in many different countries. To our good fortune, both within PricewaterhouseCoopers and among professional friends and colleagues worldwide we have had access to an enormous wealth of experience and intellect. In this section, we wish to record our gratitude to the following PricewaterhouseCoopers subject matter experts, each of whom contributed to a specific chapter:

CHAPTER 1:
THREE TIERS

Bethann B. Brault, Executive Director, Genesis Park (United States)

Hans J. C. A. Gortemaker, Eurofirm Leader, Assurance &
Business Advisory Services (Netherlands)

Rodger G. Hughes, United Kingdom Leader, Assurance &
Business Advisory Services (United Kingdom)

Jorge R. Manoel, South and Central America Theatre
Leader, Assurance & Business Advisory Services (Brazil)

John J. O'Connor, United States Leader, Assurance &
Business Advisory Services (United States)

John G. Thorn, Asia Pacific Theatre Leader, Assurance &
Business Advisory Services (Australia)

Chapter 2:
Accounting Standards

William E. Decker, Global Leader, Global Capital Markets
Group (United States)

Robert H. Herz, Retired Partner (United States)

E. Mary Keegan, Chairman, United Kingdom Accounting
Standards Board and former PricewaterhouseCoopers
Partner (United Kingdom)

Chapter 3:
Industry Standards

Willem L. J. Bröcker, Managing Partner, Global Markets
(Netherlands)

J. Frank Brown, Global Leader, Assurance & Business
Advisory Services (United States)

Chapter 4:
Good Management

Ian Coleman, Global Leader, Valuation and Strategy
(United Kingdom)

Brian J. Kinman, United States Champion, ValueReporting
(United States)
Juan A. Pujadas, Global and United States Global Risk
Management Solutions Financial Services Leader
(United States)

CHAPTER 5:
CORPORATE REPORTING

Sung-Sik Hwang, Asia Pacific Theatre Champion,
ValueReporting (South Korea)
David M. H. Phillips, European Theatre Champion,
ValueReporting (United Kingdom)
Lisa J. Stewart, Australia Champion, ValueReporting
(Australia)

CHAPTER 6:
THE INTERNET

Eric E. Cohen, XBRL Technical Leader (United States)
Bruno Tesnière, PricewaterhouseCoopers Global XBRL
Co-Leader (Belgium)
R. Michael Willis, Founding XBRL Chairman and
PricewaterhouseCoopers Global XBRL Co-Leader
(United States)

CHAPTER 7:
FUTURE AUDITS

Richard R. Kilgust, Global and United States Public Policy
and Regulatory Leader (United States)
Ellen H. Masterson, Global and United States Assurance
Methodology Leader and Global Leader,
ValueReporting (United States)

David C. Morris, Global Independence Leader, Global
    ABAS Professional, Technical Risk & Quality Leader
    (United Kingdom)

These colleagues are not responsible for errors of fact
or judgment that may remain in this book despite our best
efforts. Such things are the authors' only.

Acknowledgments

In addition to the subject matter experts whose participation in this book we must again acknowledge, we are grateful to many partners, staff members, and friends of PricewaterhouseCoopers for their contributions. Without their knowledge and help, the intensive period of thinking and writing from which this book has emerged would have been a burden. With their help, it was a time of fellowship and shared purpose.

To begin, we would like to thank Rich Baird and Joel Kurtzman for the critical role they played as project managers and in providing us constructive criticism and ideas. Mark Friedlich and Roger Lipsey, in the firm's Global Thought Leadership and Innovation group, helped us maintain high standards of quality in a book written in a short period of time.

The message of this book was shaped and refined by a number of people who are highly skilled in communication, design, marketing and publication management including Mike Ascolese, Tom Craren, Katherine D'Urso,

Peter Horowitz, Mike Kelley, Rocco Maggiotto, Tess Mateo, Amanda Merritt, Karl Pfalzgraf, and Kristen Staples. All of the exhibits were done by The Design Group of PricewaterhouseCoopers in Melbourne, Australia.

We benefited from the insights of a number of experts spanning a range of industries and functional specialties. These friends of the project include David Adair, Eleanor Andrews, Erica Baird, Bob Bertolini, Doug Chambers, Pete Collins, Ken Dakdduk, Rodger Davis, Karel De Baere, Reiner Dickmann, Miles Everson, Claire Fargeot, Patrick Frotiee, Joel Gazes, Graham Gilmour, Paul Hainsworth, Jim Harrington, Jim Gerson, Helle Bank Jorgensen, Art Karacsony, Bill Kirst, Bob Moritz, Eric Ooi, Robbie Pound, Phil Rivett, Jens Roder, Brett Savill, Rick Steinberg, Clifford Tompsett, Allen Weltmann, Joachim Wolbert, and Ian Wright.

To contribute to the current public debate about how to improve our capital markets, we knew that we needed a secret weapon to meet an aggressive writing schedule. We found it in Genesis Park, an internal think tank where the best and brightest young people come from all over the world for a five-month tour of duty in order to share their ideas and creativity. The team of Jorge Anez [Colombia], Anton Esterhuizen [South Africa], Michael Gardiner [Australia], Donna Gleeson [Australia], Joanne Higham [United Kingdom], Tomasz Kobus [Poland], Jack Pullara [United States], Leanne Sardiga [United States], and Magnus Sprenger [Germany], as well as many Genesis Park alumni, proved to be just the secret weapon we needed.

We were no less reliant on the core global ValueReporting team astutely assembled by Dave Kochanowsky: Marc Bailleux, Steve Dure, Janice Lingwood, Melissa Luo, Alison Thomas, Ton van Bree, Adriano Vargas, David Whiston, Roger Wilkes, and Matt Wissell.

Conversations with a number of people at Nasdaq challenged our thinking and helped us to clarify our positions and ideas. We would like to thank Charles Balfour, Al Berkeley, Jackie Brody, Mandana Chaffa, Barbara Cosgriff, Dan Crowley, Tad Davis, Bill Harts, Tania Kerno, Ed Knight, Maggie Kelly, Vi Lilly, Mike Sanderson, Bethany Sherman, Denise Stires, Steve Storch, Paul Warburg, David Warren, David Weild, and Wick Simmons, author of the book's Foreword.

Many other friends of PricewaterhouseCoopers were generous with their time and ideas, including John Baily, Partha Bose, Art Brody, John Clarkeson, Sally Evans, Walter Hamscher, Ray Mullady, Scott Newquist, Kathy Wallman, Steve Wallman, Don Warren, and Diana Weiss.

Once again, we are pleased to be working with the team at John Wiley & Sons, including Larry Alexander, Jeff Brown, Robert Chiarelli, Sheck Cho, Peter Knapp, and Colleen Scollan.

And once again we owe a special debt of thanks to Max Russell, the professional writer who offers us lesson after lesson in the craft of communication as he continues to help our organization bring its message to the public.

We are grateful to our wives, Melody DiPiazza and Anne Laurin Eccles—and to the Eccles' children, Charlotte, Philippa, Isabelle, and Gordon—for their patience and understanding. They accepted with grace and good humor many nights and weekends on their own. We each plan to repay many times over the debt we owe them.

SAMUEL A. DIPIAZZA JR.
ROBERT G. ECCLES

Contents

PROLOGUE

◆

PUBLIC TRUST

Enron: The largest market cap company in business history to go bankrupt. Despite headline news coverage all over the world, it will be years before the full story is known. Even then, new interpretations of this watershed event are sure to appear.

Clear beyond doubt is that this business failure has captured the attention of the public. The cast of this contemporary drama includes senior executives, directors, accountants, lawyers, sell-side analysts, accounting standard setters, rating agencies, market regulators, business trading partners, employees, banks, investment banks, and large and small investors. Billions of dollars in value have been lost, and questions are being asked about how much of that value was real in the first place. The consequences have been enormous in jobs lost, money lost, retirements in jeopardy, and sullied reputations of many innocent people who did nothing wrong except to work for or do business with Enron. Not surprisingly, many accusations are being made, many lawsuits have been filed, and proposals for new regulations and laws are under review in many countries.

Yet the awakening brought about by this genuinely tragic event promises much of value. Enron is the proverbial straw that broke the camel's back. There were precursor events—well-publicized business failures in a number of countries, the collapse of the Internet bubble, and declines, volatility, and nervousness in the equity markets due to a host of factors, all quite independent of the Enron bankruptcy. But Enron was the last straw. Attention is now focused on the virtues and flaws in the capital markets, which are more than ever recognized by the public as the foundation for value creation all over the world.

Public trust has been shaken in the institutions on which this value creation depends. These institutions share a collective responsibility for producing the information on which people of many kinds—investors, lenders, trading partners, customers, employees—depend to make a wide range of economic decisions. The challenge now is to institute the necessary reforms to ensure that public trust does not disappear, and the foundation for those reforms lies in corporate reporting.

REEXAMINING THE CORPORATE REPORTING SUPPLY CHAIN

The *Corporate Reporting Supply Chain* begins with company executives, who prepare the financial statements that are reported to investors and other stakeholders. These financial statements are approved by an independent board of directors, attested to by an independent auditing firm, analyzed by sell-side analysts, and broadcast by information distributors, including data vendors and the news media. Investors and other stakeholders then make their decisions. Standard setters and market regulators establish the roles and responsibilities of many, although certainly not all, of the participants in the Corporate Reporting Supply Chain. Enabling technologies of many kinds are used by all participants.

The time has come to reexamine how the Corporate Reporting Supply Chain works and how it can be improved. This can only be done by stepping back from the drama of the moment, yet using the event as a catalyst for reflection. Business failure will always exist in free capital markets—even the best corporate reporting will not make this go away. Improved reporting can, however, reduce the number and consequences of business failures when it enables management, the board, and the market to respond more quickly.

KEY ELEMENTS OF PUBLIC TRUST

The Enron bankruptcy is not the most important issue. Instead, it is how the aftermath of this business failure can serve as a lens to sharpen our collective focus on the key elements that create public trust in markets and, therefore, allow those markets to allocate capital efficiently. These elements are easy enough to describe, but not always easy to practice.

SPIRIT OF TRANSPARENCY

The first element is a *spirit of transparency*. Corporations have an obligation to provide willingly to shareholders and other stakeholders the information needed to make decisions. Corporations are simply the people who work in and manage them, while the board of directors of the corporation exists to ensure that the interests of shareholders are well served.

For various reasons, management and boards are not consistently making available information that they know investors would want. Too often, this failure is based on the mistaken belief that playing *The Earnings Game*—managing and beating the market's expectations about next period's earnings—will increase shareholder value. Sometimes business leaders want to hide such issues as compensation policies and conflicts of interest, which they know would not meet public approval if they became visible.

Today, shareholders and other stakeholders are demanding a much higher level of transparency. Recognizing that transparency is necessary to create and protect value, they will no longer accept being left in the dark. Financial institutions have a special responsibility here because of their role in allocating both equity and debt capital on which companies depend for their growth. Financial institutions must demand transparency from companies in order to improve this capital allocation process. What should be obvious is that they must practice what they demand of others. The cost to financial institutions of poor information is a high one; they have a very real incentive to foster a spirit of transparency in the markets as a whole.

CULTURE OF ACCOUNTABILITY

The second element is a *culture of accountability*. Providing information is not enough. It must be accompanied by a firm commitment to accountability among direct participants in the Corporate Reporting Supply Chain and those who define how it should work. Commitment means taking responsibility, and this can only occur when an ethos exists that values and understands accountability. This accountability is collective: Every member of the Corporate Reporting Supply Chain must also commit to collaborating with all others. This chain is only as strong as its weakest link. Management must hold itself accountable for using shareholders' money to make decisions that will create value for those shareholders. Independent boards exist to see that this accountability is recognized and maintained by both management and the board itself.

Accounting firms are responsible for providing assurance on certain of the information that management produces and reports. In addition, accounting firms are responsible for never forgetting that their work serves the interests of shareholders, not just the company that writes the check.

Analysts are responsible for using the reported information to produce high-quality research that investors can use to inform their decisions. Further, analysts are responsible for providing research that is free from any bias due to economic conflicts of interest.

Standard setters are responsible for establishing principles and rules for making this information useful and reliable. Regulators are responsible for ensuring that all of these groups fulfill their roles, and through careful oversight regulators are responsible for proactively identifying problems. Information distributors are responsible for making sure that information they cite or analyze from corporate reporting sources is delivered without distortion to the public. Hardware and software vendors need to be constantly monitoring and introducing useful new technologies.

Finally, investors must bear the ultimate responsibility for obtaining, understanding, and analyzing the information they use as they make personal judgments about risk and return and invest accordingly. Today, investors and other stakeholders are *demanding* greater accountability from those on whom they depend for information. Yet they must hold themselves ultimately accountable for their decisions and avoid investments where full information is unavailable or their understanding of available information has gaps.

PEOPLE OF INTEGRITY

But even transparency and accountability are not enough to establish public trust. In the end, both depend on *people of integrity*. Rules, regulations, laws, concepts, structures, processes, best practices, and the most progressive use of technology cannot ensure transparency and accountability. This can only come about when individuals of integrity are trying to "do the right thing," not what is expedient or even necessarily what is permissible. What matters in the end are the actions of people, not simply their words. Doing the right thing cannot be compromised, especially through actions that purport to create value for shareholders, but which ultimately betray them. Without personal integrity as the foundation for reported information, there can be no public trust.

THE FUTURE OF CORPORATE REPORTING

This book offers a vision of the future of corporate reporting—a vision based on a revised model of corporate disclosure, a fresh view of the responsibilities of every participant in the Corporate Reporting Supply Chain, and certain suggestions about the technology that can help make vision become reality. This vision requires significant and, in some respects, painful changes from every participant in the world's capital markets. But what this book proposes is not a rigid formula; rather it is a basis for searching dialogue among all participants in the Corporate Reporting Supply Chain. If this book spurs action toward the reforms that will build public trust, it will have accomplished its mission.

CHAPTER ONE

THREE TIERS

Information is the lifeblood of the capital markets. Investors risk their hard-earned capital in the markets in great measure based on information they receive from their target companies. They need reliable information on a timely basis. They want it in language they can understand, and they should receive it in formats they can easily use for analysis.

When the information comes from companies, investors need confidence that it is complete, accurate, and trustworthy. Management, an independent board of directors, and independent auditing firms—supported by accounting standard setters and market regulators—have specific yet interrelated responsibilities for ensuring the highest quality information possible. Investors and others have a specific responsibility as well—ensuring high-quality analysis of the information they receive.

Investors understand that in free capital markets the opportunity for gain comes with the possibility of loss. But investors have the right to expect that the benefits or consequences will result from the decisions they make, not from flawed information. Similarly, many other stakeholders make important decisions—for example, whether to work for or do business with a company—using information that companies report. Such stakeholders also need complete, accurate, and trustworthy information and they too must take responsibility for any necessary analysis.

Since the equity markets peaked in early 2000, events all over the world have shaken public confidence in the quality of reported information. A number of corporate failures and scandals have undermined the very trust investors place in those responsible for reporting that information. For markets to function efficiently and effectively, the *Corporate Reporting Supply Chain*—company executives, boards of directors, information distributors, independent auditing firms, third-party analysts, standard setters, and market regulators—along with enabling technologies for producing and consuming information must be dependable. Exhibit 1.1 illustrates and explains this supply chain concept more fully.

The need for more and better information, now heightened by a lack of trust, has led to a much more insistent demand for greater corporate transparency. Investors want greater transparency not only from companies and boards of directors, but also from independent auditors about their relationships with their audit clients. Investors want greater transparency from sell-side analysts about their compensation, potential conflicts, and how they do their work. They want the same clarity from standard setters and market regulators about how they make and enforce rules. With these calls for greater transparency come demands that all of these groups and individuals be held to higher standards of accountability.

Exhibit 1.1
The Corporate Reporting Supply Chain

| Company Executives | Boards of Directors | Independent Auditors | Information Distributors | Third-Party Analysts | Investors & Other Stakeholders |

| Standard Setters |
| Market Regulators |
| Enabling Technologies |

This simplified diagram of the Corporate Reporting Supply Chain appears throughout this book to illustrate the roles and relationships among the various groups and individuals involved in the production, preparation, communication, and use of corporate reporting information. Some of the "links" in the chain–company executives and boards of directors–require no explanation. They have the responsibility for preparing or approving the information that companies report. Other terms used to describe participants in the supply chain deserve some clarification.

- **Independent auditors,** called both auditing firms and accounting firms in this book, refers to the firms that provide independent audit opinions on the majority of the financial statements issued by publicly listed companies worldwide.

- **Information distributors** refers to data vendors that consolidate reported information and provide it for others to use. This group also includes news media, Web sites, and other communications media that provide commentary on or otherwise pass along information from or about companies.

- **Third-party analysts** refers to those who use the information reported by companies, usually in combination with other information and research, to evaluate a company's prospects and performance. In this book, the term refers most often to sell-side analysts who write research reports and issue recommendations on stock purchases to individual and institutional investors.

(continued)

- **Investors and other stakeholders** are the ultimate consumers of corporate reporting information. Investors includes company shareholders but may also refer to those who are contemplating stock purchases. Other stakeholders refers to the myriad other users of reported information including company employees, business partners, vendors, and suppliers. It also includes community members, social and environmental groups, and other nongovernmental organizations (NGOs) that may have a stake in a company's performance.

- **Standard setters** refers most often to the organizations that set accounting and auditing standards. It also includes, as this book describes, other organizations, professional associations, and industry trade groups that may play a role in setting standards or defining corporate performance measures.

- **Market regulators** includes national governmental agencies, territorial coalitions, transnational bodies, and even stock exchanges that set and enforce rules relating to corporate reporting. Legislative bodies play a role here as well

- **Enabling technologies** is used here primarily to refer to Internet technologies and Extensible Business Reporting Language (XBRL), in particular, that enable the widespread distribution and use of reported information both inside and outside of companies. They also refer to hardware and software developed by technology companies for collecting and analyzing information.

Investors are not alone. Lenders, customers, suppliers, employees, and nongovernmental organizations (NGOs) have added their voices to the cry for transparency. The information-based decisions of all of these stakeholders affect investors because they can affect a company's stock price.

Executives and boards will serve their enlightened self-interests by heeding the cry for greater transparency. Price-waterhouseCoopers research has shown that investors, analysts, and executives themselves all believe that better disclosure can have significant benefits for companies: more long-term investors, greater analyst following, improved access to new capital and a lower cost of capital, increased management credibility, greater management accountability, and higher share prices.[1]

Higher share prices clearly benefit shareholders when they are based on real value creation—and not on the management of earnings expectations and reported earnings. When value creation is real, the size and liquidity of the markets are more likely to increase on a sustained basis and result in more wealth not only for shareholders, but also for society as a whole.

MOVEMENT TOWARD GREATER TRANSPARENCY

Many companies in the marketplace have been dedicated for many years to a spirit of transparency and openness. This book offers more than a few examples. For instance, some companies are providing better segment information or working to make financial statements easier to understand. Some companies go beyond regulatory requirements and report nonfinancial information that offers the investor a richer and more accurate company profile. This nonfinancial information includes performance on "value drivers" that are the basis for future financial results—for example, effective customer relationship management, development of human capital, and improvements in the innovation process.

Other companies provide forward-looking information to give investors insights into management's view of the future. Still more use the Internet not only to present financial statements, but also to post executives' speeches and to include individual investors in Web-based conference calls. Alongside this electronic channel, members of the management team are making themselves more available for direct discussions with investors and other stakeholders.

Boards of directors are beginning to look harder at companies' internal control and risk management systems. Auditing firms continue to improve their methodologies for providing assurance on reported financial statements. Firms that provide sell-side research are taking steps to eliminate any conflicts of interest and to ensure the quality of the research they publish.

Standard setters are examining whether existing accounting standards provide the necessary information in a way that is useful to investors. Market regulators are looking harder at the roles played by all of these groups to ensure that each holds itself accountable for properly fulfilling its role.

A NEW MODEL FOR CORPORATE TRANSPARENCY

Despite the many ongoing efforts to improve how the markets function, each group involved has its own goals and its own rather narrow view of what will make things better. The market requires a larger organizing framework that will focus all of these efforts on the overarching goal of ensuring that investors and other stakeholders get the information they need to make appropriate decisions.

Exhibit 1.2 offers such a framework. The *Three-Tier Model of Corporate Transparency* is one alternative for a new vision of the future of corporate reporting. Much is being done today to make each of these tiers a reality, and suggestions for how to accelerate this progress are included in this book.

The model's three tiers include:

1. A set of truly global generally accepted accounting principles (Global GAAP).

2. Standards for measuring and reporting information that are industry-specific, consistently applied, and developed by the industries themselves.

3. Guidelines for company-specific information such as strategy, plans, risk management practices, compensation policies, corporate governance, and performance measures unique to the company.

Exhibit 1.2
The Three-Tier Model of Corporate Transparency

The Three-Tier Model does not ask companies simply to report information in three disconnected tiers. Investors and other stakeholders will benefit fully only if companies communicate the information in each tier in an integrated fashion that provides a holistic view of the enterprise—its marketplace opportunities, its strategies and their implementation, its value drivers, and its financial outcomes. Chapter 5 presents one model for doing this, the *Value-Reporting™ Framework.*

The following paragraphs offer a more thorough discussion of what the three tiers mean, including how the elements in each tier can change. Tier-Three information can move to Tier Two and Tier-Two information can move to Tier One. Beyond these shifts, the opportunity will always exist to add more information at Tier Three.

TIER ONE: GLOBAL GENERALLY ACCEPTED ACCOUNTING PRINCIPLES

Companies today use a wide variety of generally accepted accounting principles (GAAP) for reporting their financial results. Many different forms of country-based GAAP exist, such as those of Australia, Germany, Japan, the United Kingdom, and the United States. The closest the corporate reporting world has come to Global GAAP is the International Financial Reporting Standards (IFRS), formerly named International Accounting Standards, which will be mandatory for all listed companies in the European Union by the year 2005.[2] Chapter 2 discusses the key issues that must be addressed in creating Global GAAP, including the important and complicated matter of how to gain acceptance for it in the United States.

A compelling argument can be made for Global GAAP as the foundation for the future of corporate reporting. Just as markets for tangible products have become global, so have the capital markets. Companies want access to capital markets all over the world because they want to tap into large pools of liquidity—such as on the exchanges in London (10 percent nondomestic listings), Nasdaq (15 percent nondomestic), or New York (19 percent nondomestic).[3] Others wish to use their stock to make acquisitions in foreign countries where the company does business. While more and more companies want access to the world's capital markets, without a global set of generally accepted accounting principles the process of getting there is very difficult and expensive.

Market regulators and the stock exchanges they oversee impose a variety of rules regarding the appropriate set of accounting standards companies must use in local markets. They often require a listed company to convert to the host country's GAAP, U.S. GAAP, or to International Financial Reporting Standards. Others require companies to reconcile their local GAAP results to standards acceptable to the host country.

For example, non-U.S. companies that want to list in the United States must either convert their results to U.S. GAAP or use other recognized standards reconciled to U.S. GAAP. The lack of Global GAAP results in frictional costs that impair a company's ability to gain access to global pools of capital.

Investors also bear their share of the problems. Just as companies want access to capital around the world, investors wish to invest around the world. But the vast differences that exist among national and international accounting standards, and in the levels of transparency they create, impair the ability of investors to compare the financial performance of companies that report according to different sets of standards.

Differences also exist in how rigorously executives and their boards apply these standards in creating their financial statements, how independent accounting firms audit them, and how market regulators enforce adherence to them. When accounting standards and the rigor with which they have been enforced are suspect, companies pay a very real price. Uncertainty about the reliability of reported financial information can be reflected in a higher cost of capital through a lower share price. Investors will demand a greater return in order to compensate for the higher level of risk caused by greater uncertainty about the quality of the information provided. This has happened to a number of companies in the United States when declines in stock prices have followed closely on the heels of questions about the quality of revenues or earnings.

The negative consequences of incomplete and unreliable information can extend well beyond an individual company or even stock market. They can affect an entire economy. In an analysis of the Asian crisis, the International Monetary Fund (IMF) reported that "although private sector expenditure and financing decisions led to the crisis, it was made worse by governance issues, notably government involvement in the private sector and lack of transparency in corporate and fiscal accounting and the provision of financial and economic data."[4]

If Global GAAP existed, investors could much more easily and accurately compare the performance of any company, in any country, in any industry. This would vastly broaden their investment choices because they could avoid the difficulty and costs of comparing company performance and assessing risk across different types of GAAP. Risks due to a country's economic and political situation, the quality of governance and market regulation, and the company's industry dynamics would still exist, but at least an investor would have reliable and comparable information on any company of interest.

At Tier One, market regulators worldwide would agree to allow any company using Global GAAP to list on the exchanges within their jurisdictions. At their discretion, they could decide whether or not to make Global GAAP mandatory for domestic companies or even for all companies that seek access to public or private capital. In some circumstances, a preferable approach might be to let some companies continue using local GAAP—private companies or publicly listed small and medium-sized enterprises. However, those publicly listed companies that did not also produce Global GAAP financial statements would eventually find capital in other parts of the world difficult to access and expensive.

TIER TWO: INDUSTRY-BASED STANDARDS

An obvious impact of globalization is that companies within any given industry increasingly compete with their counterparts in other countries. Further, the competitive dynamics of specific industries, how those industries create value for shareholders, and the knowledge needed to create value vary widely across different industries. What other stakeholders want to know also varies across industries. For example, environmental and social NGOs want different types of information about oil and gas companies (e.g., environmental impact) as compared to the information they want about apparel manufacturing companies (e.g., labor practices in developing countries).

Assume that an investor has decided to invest in a particular industry. The next decision is to choose among companies within that industry, and this naturally requires comparing one company's performance to that of its competitors. Global GAAP provides a foundation for this type of comparative analysis, but a standard set of accounting principles is not enough. Investors need supplemental information, both financial and nonfinancial, to gain a more complete view of a company's past performance and to make inferences about its future prospects. Examples of supplemental financial information include pro forma earnings and free cash flow, neither of which is covered by any form of GAAP. Examples of nonfinancial information include performance measures relating to intellectual capital and environmental pollution. Even for the same measure, the methodology used can vary substantially across industries. Banks, for example, do not measure customer satisfaction in the same way that hospitals do.

PricewaterhouseCoopers research in a broad range of industries shows conclusively that what drives value differs dramatically across industries. Chapter 3 offers a brief comparison between the telecommunications and pharmaceutical industries to illustrate such differences.

Global investors are not alone in their need to compare a company's performance with others'. Executives must compare their companies with peers in other countries to evaluate the competitive landscape. For example, a money center bank in London that competes globally for corporate or retail customers needs to compare its performance to competitors in Frankfurt, New York, and Tokyo. Predominantly, it needs to make relevant comparisons based on information about the value drivers specific to banking.

That is where the difficulty begins. Companies within the same industry report industry-specific value driver information in an uneven fashion due to the lack of universally accepted definitions, measurement methodologies, and reporting conventions. Even if many companies in an industry reported on an important piece of nonfinancial information—such as customer retention in banking and insurance or market growth and market share in high technology or telecommunications—the usefulness of this information would be limited if one company's set of numbers could not be compared to those of others.

To make such industry-specific information—the domain of Tier Two—truly useful to both investors and companies, standards are needed. Ideally, these standards will be developed by global, industry-based groups such as trade associations in collaboration with others in the Corporate Reporting Supply Chain, including the investor community, analysts, professional services firms, and independent accountants.

To create an incentive for this to happen and to prevent liability concerns from inhibiting transparency, regulation and legislation that provide "safe harbor" legal protection to companies reporting according to these standards should apply. Companies that provide useful forward-looking information to investors, explicitly identified as such, should not be penalized for doing so.

Although certainly not a widespread movement yet, examples can be found of industry-based groups that have proposed what could be considered Tier-Two measurement standards. The Society of Petroleum Engineers and the World Petroleum Congress, for example, have jointly developed a set of principles for petroleum reserves and encourages companies to use them; although the developers say that the principles "should not in any manner be construed to be compulsory or obligatory."[5] In the hotel industry, the *Uniform System of Accounts for the Lodging Industry,* a uniform accounting and financial reporting system for hotels, has noted "revenue per available room (RevPAR)" as an industry-specific measure with suggested methods of calculation.[6]

Even though Tier-Two standards will be developed at the industry level, the possibility certainly exists that some of them could eventually be incorporated into Tier One. For example, certain financial measures of risk and value might be developed in several industries that would be useful in many others. Independently developed industry standards might be similar enough that they could form the basis for new standards within Global GAAP.

TIER THREE: COMPANY-SPECIFIC INFORMATION

Assuming that both Global GAAP and global industry standards existed for all key financial and nonfinancial measures, investors and other stakeholders would still need a great deal of information specific to an individual company. This information might include:

- Management's view of its competitive environment, including opportunities and threats.
- Strategies the company has chosen to exploit opportunities to create value for shareholders, as well as plans for implementing these strategies.
- The value drivers—and results information on them— that are uniquely important to the company although not covered by Tier-One or Tier-Two standards.

- Qualitative and quantitative targets, both absolute and benchmarked to a defined group of peers.
- The company's desired risk profile and how it manages upside and downside risks.
- The company's internal control and compliance procedures.
- The company's compensation policies.
- The company's principles of corporate governance.
- The commitments of the company to stakeholders other than shareholders.

This constitutes Tier-Three information, the foundation of good management as discussed in Chapter 4. By definition, Tier-Three information is unique to a specific company. Therefore, a company must decide how much of the Tier-Three information to report publicly. While well-defined external standards cannot be developed for Tier-Three content, general guidelines for content, as well as external standards for the format of reporting such information, certainly can be developed.

This is already happening. For example, the U.K. Accounting Standards Board (ASB) has issued (for comment) recommended revisions in a company's operating and financial review (OFR) statements, known as "management discussion and analysis" in the United States.[7] The draft proposes that a company's board of directors should discuss the objectives of the business and the strategy for achieving those objectives, as well as identify and comment on the measures used as key performance indicators in managing the business. Consistent with the spirit of Tier Two, the ASB also emphasizes the importance of defining and disclosing both financial and nonfinancial measures widely used within the industry sector.

Conceivably, in addition to such content guidelines, standard-setting bodies could develop format guidelines concerning how to use the Internet for reporting information, how often it should be updated, and rules under which it should be disclosed. For example, in the United States, Regulation Fair Disclosure, enacted in October 2000, stipulates that all analysts and investors must be provided with material information at the same time instead of in a selective or privileged way as had been done in the past.[8]

Just as Tier-Two information can move to Tier One, Tier-Three information could move to Tier Two. An example would be an individual company that starts reporting information on what it believes to be an important new value driver. Other companies might feel compelled to do the same, using their own measurement methodologies. If the market found this information useful, but not as useful as it would be if it were truly comparable across companies, investors would exert pressure for industry-wide, comparable standards to be created. Once this happened, information on this value driver would then become Tier-Two information.

Finally, the future of corporate reporting is inevitably moving toward greater transparency. Companies will continue to innovate and experiment with new types and new formats of information reported at Tier Three.

THREE TIERS OF ASSURANCE

Providing assurance on the information companies report follows directly from the nature of the standards upon which the information is based. At Tier One, assurance would be mandatory for any company using Global GAAP. It would be provided by an independent group, like the established auditing firms, which has the requisite credibility in the eyes of companies and the public.

Initially, getting assurance on Tier-Two information should be voluntary in the same way that using Tier-Two standards should be voluntary. The market would then decide the value of having an independent party assure that the reported numbers were prepared according to the applicable set of standards. Of course, regulators could always decide to make assurance mandatory and would likely do so if they made certain reporting standards mandatory.

Over time, a combination of marketplace and regulatory forces would probably lead to mandatory assurance. Firms or individuals with the necessary skills, capabilities, and credibility, acceptable to regulators, would provide the assurance. In addition to auditing firms, this broad peer group could include general strategy consulting firms, industry-specific consulting firms, and IT service providers and systems integrators. Every candidate member of this group would also have to satisfy high standards of independence, as is true for the independent auditing firms today, for an assurance opinion to *be* and to *be perceived* as truly objective.

Because standards would exist, auditing Tier-Two information would be similar to auditing Tier-One information. In some cases, an industry association could contribute significantly to this audit, for example, by producing information assured by an independent third party, on market size and market share for use by all companies within the sector. Tier-Two audits would not be identical to those at Tier One, however, because at least initially the standards would not be expressed in an integrated framework like Global GAAP.

As at Tier Two, assurance on Tier-Three information would at first be voluntary. It could, however, become mandatory and become a service offered by firms and individuals that had the requisite expertise, credibility, and independence. The great difference at Tier Three lies in the nature of the assurance provided. Tier-Three assurance on reported information would focus on answering questions such as: Did management actually do what it reported? Was the company's externally reported strategy the same as its internally reported one? Were the risk management practices the company described actually applied? Was the externally reported performance metric the same one that management used internally? When comparative figures were given over time or across business units, did the company consistently apply the same set of internal standards?

Tier-Three assurance involves a high level of judgment since much of it concerns the behavioral aspects of management. In some cases, a company might choose to report only information on which the assurance provider is willing to agree, and no more. In such an instance, the quality of the information reported would be assured, but completeness of information might still be lacking.

This points out a significant challenge for assurance at Tier Three: the very real risk that management will only provide "positive" information. If other important, albeit less positive, information goes unreported, the value of an assurance opinion at Tier Three should be suspect. The firm providing assurance at Tier Three would no doubt want to include in its opinion its assessment of the reported information's completeness. Important categories missing information would need to be identified for the opinion to be most useful.

From content to format

Format counts. Even the most accurate, relevant, and complete information would be all but useless for management decisions if it were presented on stone tablets at corporate headquarters. The same is true for information reported to investors and other stakeholders.

Traditionally, accounting standards have focused on the content of the information that companies should provide to the public. In adopting the Three-Tier Model and reporting on more information, much of it new or very different, equal attention should be paid to the format in which this content is communicated and subsequently consumed by investors, analysts, and other stakeholders.

Not long ago, the format for information was not really subject to choice; it was paper or nothing at all. Even with today's electronic technology, most content is still reported in formats that are very little more than electronic versions of paper, for example, the pdf format for annual reports found on Web sites.

The opportunity now exists for companies to report the information they provide to the public using an Internet-enabled platform called Extensible Business Reporting Language (XBRL®), one of the key enabling technologies in the Corporate Reporting Supply Chain (Exhibit 1.3). XBRL will play an essential role in achieving the corporate transparency embodied in the Three-Tier Model because of its ability to "tag" any individual piece of information with a precise contextual description. Such self-describing information will greatly facilitate the access and use of information by investors, while at the same time enhancing their ability to validate the reported information in accordance with prescribed standards, such as Global GAAP at Tier One and industry-based standards at Tier Two.

Exhibit 1.3
Enabling Technologies in the
Corporate Reporting Supply Chain

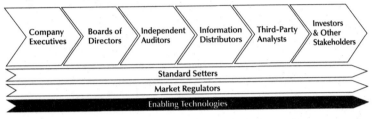

Chapter 6 explores in more detail how XBRL will revolutionize the Corporate Reporting Supply Chain. However, because the content of the information at all three tiers is currently constrained by the pervasive paper-based formats used today, further discussion of the three tiers should not proceed without a basic understanding of how the Internet and XBRL will yield significant improvements in:

- The quality of the information being used.
- The speed and frequency with which information can be prepared, reported, and used.
- The usefulness of the information.
- The completeness of the information used in analysis.

QUALITY OF INFORMATION

Significant quality problems can arise because of transposition and other errors made when taking information from electronic or paper documents and reentering it into analytical applications. In XBRL, such errors are all but eliminated. Validation processes inherent in XBRL documents result in information that is more accurate and internally consistent. XBRL also allows investors and other stakeholders to verify that the source from which they obtained the information is in fact its true source, eliminating the problem of "misinformation," for example, from a bogus press release sent out by an imposter.

SPEED AND FREQUENCY

XBRL will dramatically increase the speed at which users can obtain information. Users will no longer have to rely on their web browsers to search out the information they want. When information is tagged in XBRL, stakeholders can simply make an information request from within their analytical software and in seconds the information or data they want will be incorporated into their analysis. Such tools can quickly find and extract information—for example, a company's revenue recognition policy, buried in the footnotes of a 100-page annual report—and present only the specific information that the investor wants to analyze.

XBRL also speeds the company's access to its own information. Some companies have well-oiled internal systems and processes for accessing and using critical information. XBRL can further reduce internal barriers to consolidating information, thus making information sharing among disparate internal data warehouses much easier.

Although companies can certainly post and update information on their Web sites today, making information available on a "continuous reporting" basis is very difficult in a paper-based reporting environment. With XBRL, investors would gain immediate access to information as frequently as companies make it available. The choice of how frequently a company might choose to report, however, would depend on the relative importance of the information to stakeholders and how frequently management updates this information for its own use.

MORE USEFUL INFORMATION

Information is most useful when users can obtain it easily from multiple sources and use it or share it among disparate software application packages for any type of analysis. For example, investors could obtain information from a company's financial statements, compare it to similar information obtained from analysts' reports, and then pass the same information to someone else for a different type of analysis.

MORE COMPLETE INFORMATION

Finally, in an XBRL environment, investors and others will have access to much more complete information because the current high cost of accessing and consuming information will approach zero. All users will have greater access to the information that companies report, as well as to market-based information currently hidden in mountains of paper. Used properly, such information will enable better analysis by all internal and external decision makers.

IMPLICATIONS FOR THE FUTURE OF CORPORATE REPORTING

The improvements in reporting just described all stem from the fact that the XBRL format transforms electronic paper into documents that function more dynamically, as in a database. In an XBRL-enabled reporting environment and using application software packages now being developed, all investors, including the growing number of individuals who invest directly in the market, will be able to perform sophisticated analysis much more quickly and easily.

Today, the large brokerage firms and institutional investors have a significant advantage because sophisticated analysis is very paper-based and requires a great deal of labor-intensive preparation. Individual investors, especially, may not have the resources needed to do the same. XBRL will help to level the playing field by reducing the time and cost for collecting the data for analysis, which will take only a few seconds at most.

XBRL AND STANDARDS

As powerful as XBRL is, it is not a set of corporate reporting standards. XBRL depends on having reporting standards in place. The relevance and reliability of information tagged in XBRL will be no better than the standards used to create the information in the first place. The content that results from principles-based standards and the use of an XBRL-enabled format are two sides of the same coin. Both are essential to the future of corporate reporting.

NOTES

1. PricewaterhouseCoopers research refers to the aggregate results from 14 independent country surveys conducted by PricewaterhouseCoopers in 1997 and 1998. Very similar results are obtained from the ongoing PricewaterhouseCoopers industry surveys. The industry survey results are posted and updated on the ValueReporting Web site at www.valuereporting.com. For a detailed discussion on the benefits of better disclosure, see Robert G. Eccles, Robert H. Herz, E. Mary Keegan, and David M. H. Phillips, *The ValueReporting Revolution: Moving Beyond the*

Earnings Game (New York: John Wiley & Sons, 2001), 190–191, hereafter referred to as Eccles, *The ValueReporting Revolution.*

2. Companies already using U.S. GAAP as their primary basis of accounting have until 2007 to convert, as do companies that only have publicly traded debt.

3. Data source for calculating the percentages of foreign listings on the London, Nasdaq, and New York exchanges: International Federation of Stock Exchanges, www.world-exchanges .org. Data were as of February 2000.

4. External Relations Department of the International Monetary Fund, "The IMF's Response to the Asian Crisis: A Factsheet," International Monetary Fund, January 17, 1999. Also see www.imf.org/external/np/exr/facts/asia.htm.

5. Society of Petroleum Engineers, "Petroleum Reserves Definitions," April 27, 2002, www.spe.org/spe/cda/views/shared/ viewChannelsMaster/0,2883,1648_19738_19746_24741,00.html.

6. *Uniform System of Accounts for the Lodging Industry,* 9th ed., Educational Institute of the American Hotel Motel Association, November 1996.

7. U.K. Accounting Standards Board, *Revision of the Statement "Operating and Financial Review,"* exposure draft statement (London: U.K. Accounting Standards Board, June 2002).

8. U.S. Securities and Exchange Commission, "Final Rule: Selective Disclosure and Insider Trading," 17 CFR Parts 240, 243, and 249, Release Nos. 33-7881, 34-43154, IC-24599, File No. S7-31-99, RIN 3235-AH82 (New York: U.S. Securities and Exchange Commission, August 15, 2000). Also see www.sec.gov/rules/final/33-7881.htm.

CHAPTER TWO

ACCOUNTING STANDARDS

At the foundation of the Three-Tier Model of Corporate Transparency is Global GAAP, a set of accounting standards for reporting a company's financial performance for a defined period. Today, every country that has a public capital market either uses a set of local generally accepted accounting principles (GAAP) or one based on other national or international standards. The quality of these standards varies widely from country to country, as does how well they are applied by companies and eventually audited by independent accountants.

Even the best country-GAAP standards have come under criticism since they are all based for the most part on an historical cost model. Today's more complex business environment challenges the relevance of historical cost information and is putting strain on this model. The capital markets focus on value and, as discussed later, value can be substantially different from historical cost.

CRITICISMS OF GAAP TODAY

Even before the Enron bankruptcy, and still today, the critics of GAAP have been growing in number and complaining more loudly, especially in the United States. PricewaterhouseCoopers industry research shows that only about 20 percent of investors, analysts, and executives consider financial reports prepared under current GAAP as *very useful* in communicating the true value of a company. And only 60 percent, on average, view them as *fairly useful.*[1]

A *BusinessWeek* article published in 2001 states, "Many institutional investors, most Wall Street analysts, and even many accountants say GAAP is irrelevant."[2] It quotes a vocal critic of U.S. GAAP, Robert Willens (an accounting expert at Lehman Brothers, Inc.), as saying, "I don't know anyone who uses GAAP net income anymore for anything."[3] On the other hand, the proliferation of nonstandard pro forma reporting has led some to demand that pro forma results be reconciled to or reported with GAAP results. And even the harshest critics of GAAP agree that good accounting standards properly applied internally should be the foundation for performance measurement and serve as the basis for external reporting.

Criticism about GAAP worldwide falls into three broad categories. The critics say that existing GAAP:

1. Fosters *The Earnings Game* played by both management and the markets since earnings has long been the single most important measure of performance.

2. Does not account for or disclose certain types of information about intangible assets.

3. Does not communicate adequate information about value creation because it is a mixed model that

includes historical cost, amortized cost, written down cost, and fair value for certain financial instruments and other assets in some countries and industries.

EARNINGS

The criticisms related to earnings are many. Detractors say that the market focuses increasingly on cash earnings, not GAAP earnings, as the best measure of the bottom line, although cash earnings is not currently defined by GAAP. Detractors also say that GAAP does not take into account many other important drivers of value. They point out that while earnings is an important measure of performance, its importance as an indicator of future value has been declining over time.[4] Consequently, price/earnings (P/E) ratios have become a more limited guide to investors.[5]

Another major criticism is that accounting rules have multiplied and become ever more complex as GAAP standards attempt to keep pace with changes in the business environment. As a result, financial statements have become more difficult to understand and interpret. Adding to this complexity is the fact that companies have developed their own nonstandard measures of the bottom line, such as pro forma earnings (discussed in more detail in the next chapter), which they claim are a better measure of their underlying bottom-line financial performance.

INTANGIBLE ASSETS

One of the commonly cited reasons for the limited usefulness of P/E ratios is that earnings may be understated because certain intangible assets, such as research and development, are treated as current period expenses under GAAP. If these assets were capitalized on the balance sheet and amortized over time, current earnings would be higher in periods of investment.

How important are intangible assets? The ratio of the market value (value assigned to the company based on the market's expectation of future cash flow and risk) to the book value on the balance sheet (the difference between the recorded assets and liabilities of the company as of a point in time) for the Standard & Poor's 500 stood at 1.3 in the early 1980s.[6] In 1997, the same ratio was 6.5. It went down to 5.4 as the markets dropped precipitously after September 11, 2001, and stood at 4.3 as of March 31, 2002.[7]

If the historical balance sheet only captures, on average, about 20 percent of the market value of companies today, what makes up the remaining 80 percent? Intangible assets, nonfinancial value drivers, and, possibly, the difference between historical cost and market value of the assets recorded. On the other side of the "ledger" are unrecorded stock option costs and off balance sheet financings, which have received a great deal of attention lately.

More generally, examples of assets that do not show up on the balance sheet under GAAP include leased assets, assets in some special purpose entities (SPEs), and physical assets that have been completely depreciated but retain real value. This has led to calls for a *fair value* approach in which the assets would be placed on the balance sheet and valued in a way that more accurately reflects their "true" value. But critics of fair value reporting raise issues about recording the value of other assets, such as intangibles like customer loyalty or brand equity, pointing out that for many of them no reliable measurement methodologies currently exist.

THE EARNINGS GAME

GAAP does not inherently promote The Earnings Game, something easy to describe but complicated to play.[8] The game is based on the market's focus on net income, earnings per share, and the belief that increases in stock prices come from a steady and predictable track record of period-to-period earnings increases, particularly if reported earnings beat expectations. Some managers have learned how to manage the market's expectations about the next period's earnings and how to meet or slightly beat those expectations.

Critics claim that GAAP gives management too many degrees of freedom, at least for a while, to report the necessary level of earnings in any given period. They even view attempts to adjust GAAP, such as fair value accounting, as introducing yet more degrees of freedom for management to manipulate reported earnings.

Despite the global popularity of The Earnings Game, empirical studies show no relationship between meeting or beating earnings expectations and stock returns.[9] As a real-world example, consider the now-famous story of how Enron executives endeavored always to meet or beat earnings expectations, a tactic that eventually exacted great costs from the firm and its stakeholders. For 12 straight quarters, starting in the last quarter of 1998, Enron met or beat the analysts' consensus estimates. How did the market respond? In seven of those quarters, within the 24-hour period after earnings were announced Enron's stock went up; in five it declined.[10] The perceived advantages to be gained from playing The Earnings Game are little more than a market myth.

Criticizing a focus on earnings is not meant to imply that current and past earnings are not a valid measure of financial performance. Investors need to know how well management has used the capital with which it has been entrusted—this is fundamental to determining how much value has been created. Earnings are important, but investors need other financial performance measures as well. Expecting that one number can serve as an adequate report card on management's performance in any given period is unreasonable. These other financial measures, along with nonfinancial measures such as data about customer satisfaction and employee retention at Tier Two and other information at Tier Three, are important because the market looks to them for its view of the company's future cash flow, which determines its value.

GETTING TO GLOBAL GAAP

GAAP is a mixed model that includes historical cost, amortized cost, written-down cost, and fair value for certain financial instruments and other assets in some countries and industries. This model contributes to the difficulty of understanding the basic financial statements, can result in similar transactions being accounted for differently because of differing interpretations, and imposes complexity.

Getting to a set of Global GAAP standards, Tier One in the Three-Tier Model of Corporate Transparency (Exhibit 2.1), will involve confronting these issues at various levels and will require cooperation among many parties, including national standard setters, key regulators, governments, the corporate community, and the auditing profession. The central issues include:

- Agreeing on the approach to and scope of accounting standards.

Exhibit 2.1
Tier One in the Three-Tier Model of
Corporate Transparency

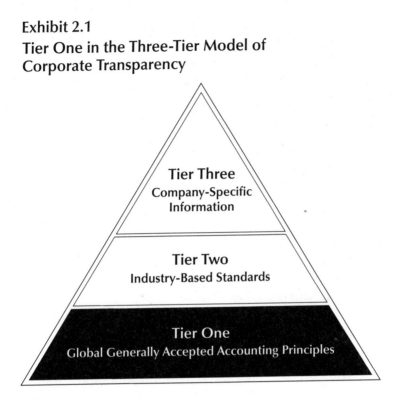

Tier Three
Company-Specific
Information

Tier Two
Industry-Based Standards

Tier One
Global Generally Accepted Accounting Principles

- Resolving fundamental conceptual debates.
- Converging specific international standards and national standards.

In addressing these issues, the parties involved should maintain an emphasis on transparency, high-quality reporting, and good corporate governance. They must also bear in mind that getting to Global GAAP will require training and education across all disciplines and functions and at all levels of responsibility.

APPROACH AND SCOPE ISSUES

To achieve the goal of Global GAAP, investors and other users of financial statements, national standard setters, key regulators, governments, the corporate community, and the auditing profession must come to agreement on the right approach to use in developing standards and on the scope of their applicability.

A major theme in the current debate regarding accounting standards revolves around "rules versus principles." U.S. GAAP is usually cited as an example of highly rules based standards (significant detail), while U.K. GAAP and the current International Financial Reporting Standards (IFRS) exemplify principles-based standards (broad guidelines).

The Enron bankruptcy in the United States has pushed this debate to the point of acrimony in some parts of the world. Frits Bolkestein, the European Union commissioner responsible for the Internal Market Taxation and Customs Union, went so far as to decry "the cookery book approach" of U.S. GAAP and has called for the United States to move to IFRS.[11]

The advocates of principles-based standards criticize the "bright lines" that get drawn in a rules-based approach. Rules that are specific and clear can lead to adhering to the letter of the standard rather than to its spirit. Knowing precisely what you must do often defines precisely what you do not have to do.

All accounting standards are based on principles. As new transactions and business models are invented in business practice—derivatives and dot-coms, for example—new standards are developed. As those who use the standards ask for clarification, rules get made. Ironically, the more clarification is sought, the more complex the rules become. Even in a principles-based model, the number of principles can increase to cover more narrow types of transactions, and as the articulation and interpretation of a standard become more detailed, principles may morph into rules.

For standards to remain true to the principles on which they are based, they must above all focus on capturing and reporting the economic substance of a transaction. Five cornerstones should underlie such standards. Principles-based standards should:

- Address issues of broad scope.
- Reflect appropriately the economic substance of transactions.
- Result in similar transactions being treated similarly.
- Contain few, if any, alternatives, exceptions, or compromises.
- Result in reporting and disclosure that are transparent and useful for decision making.

Standards built on these cornerstones start with broad principles. They provide supporting rules when necessary and explanatory guidance, including relevant examples. They need not answer every question or generate a rule for every specific instance. Any rules developed should remain consistent with the principles on which they are based, and where particular situations are not covered by specific rules, companies and auditors should look to the substance of the principle.

PUTTING PRINCIPLES INTO PRACTICE

However attractive a principles-based approach to standards is, living by it is not easy. Everybody involved—companies, accounting firms, standard setters, and regulators—must be truly committed to making it work. Company executives truly do need, in the spirit of transparency, to use these standards to provide the information they know investors want, rather than treating principles as an opportunity for obfuscation.

Auditing firms need to have a deeply embedded culture of accountability that makes them feel responsible for using their best judgment in helping clients get to "the best" rather than the "marginally acceptable" accounting treatment of a transaction. They must learn to live with a higher degree of ambiguity and avoid seeking rules that lessen their accountability, whether in relation to company executives or to investors. Finally, standard setters and market regulators should be prepared to accommodate standards that allow for, and even require, the exercise of appropriate professional judgment, recognizing that it is not possible to mandate specific rules to cover every possible situation.

GLOBAL GAAP FOR ALL COMPANIES?

Another issue on which agreement must be reached is sometimes characterized as "Big GAAP/Little GAAP." The essence of the issue is whether to develop Global GAAP standards with all companies in mind or only for those that access global and national capital markets.

In the United States, certain existing standards apply only to public companies. Two examples are *segment reporting* and *earnings per share.* Other countries—for example, Canada and the United Kingdom—have created a simplified GAAP with disclosures specific to small and medium-sized enterprises. At least at the start, the most logical choice would be global standards developed with global capital markets in mind.

Specialized industry GAAP

In the United States, the approach has been to develop highly specialized rules for many specialized industries. International and other national approaches, in general, do not have such specialization, except for financial services.

The convergence of industries into broader sectors calls into question whether the specialized U.S. approach can be maintained. Within the Three-Tier Model, the broad principles would apply to all industries, and industry-specific or activity-based standards would be developed consistent with the overall principles.

Key concepts at issue

As a next step, the following fundamental issues need to be debated among the appropriate participants in the Corporate Reporting Supply Chain and specifically addressed:

- Historical cost versus fair value.
- Reporting on financial performance.

- Reporting on intangibles.

- Defining the reporting entity.

HISTORICAL COST VERSUS FAIR VALUE

Whether to value assets at cost or at fair market value on the balance sheet is one of the more controversial conceptual debates. GAAP currently is a mixed model: Some assets are valued at historical cost, others at market or fair value. Even within a class of assets—financial instruments, for example—mixed valuation approaches exist. Generally, historical costs are used for nonmonetary items, although in many countries real estate and certain fixed assets are periodically revalued.

Few deny the usefulness to investors of having insight into the real worth of a company's assets, especially their worth from different perspectives such as replacement value, ongoing value, break-up value, and liquidation value. With such information, investors can gain a more realistic sense of the company's liquidity and solvency and how the company could meet its obligations under various scenarios. Critics say that the greater relevance of these different value scenarios is often offset by the lower reliability of measuring assets at fair value.

Critics of fair value accounting also point out that it introduces volatility in a company's earnings as values go up or down according to the external market conditions that determine value. The logical response here is that this volatility is simply an indication of the underlying economic reality and begs the question of the most appropriate way to report on fair values in the financial statements. Further, when more emphasis is based on cash flow than on earnings, the volatility in earnings should be less correlated with volatility in stock price if current and expected future cash flows have not significantly changed.

Finally, a valid but converse criticism holds that measuring assets and liabilities at fair value actually creates opportunities for management to smooth earnings, although this depends on just what assets are being valued.

One way to help improve the usefulness and comparability of fair value measures is for management to provide the key assumptions used in making its calculations. The market can then make its own assessment about how reasonable the assumptions and how accurate the calculations really are. Inherent in this is the trade-off between the greater relevance of fair value information and the greater reliability with which historical costs can be measured.

Getting the right balance here will not be easy. The subject is complicated, requiring much study and debate. Reaching a final answer in the very near term may not be a realistic expectation, but as new analytical techniques are developed and as different types of markets merge, what remains difficult to measure at fair value today could be more easily done in the future.

REPORTING ON FINANCIAL PERFORMANCE

The International Accounting Standards Board (IASB) and the U.K. Accounting Standards Board (ASB) have a joint project, and the Financial Accounting Standards Board (FASB) in the United States is doing similar work on financial performance reporting to consider how better to display the elements in the income statement as well as those that comprise comprehensive income. This includes grouping like items together in terms of the similarity of their underlying persistence and use in forecasting. It also includes consideration of whether standard definitions should be developed for such measures as operating income and earnings before interest, taxes, depreciation, and amortization (EBITDA). Further, the project will consider better ways to display cash flow definitions for measures like *free cash flow* and *cash earnings*.

This project is especially important if there is a general movement toward more fair value measurement. Separating out value changes from ongoing accrual-based earnings in the income statement will provide useful information and may reduce some of the concern about the volatility associated with fair value measurement.

REPORTING ON INTANGIBLES

Standards for reporting on intangibles vary significantly among geographies. Under IFRS, companies can capitalize more intangibles on the balance sheet (generally on a cost basis) than under U.S. GAAP. Under no current standards, however, can companies include separately on the balance sheet items such as intellectual capital, know-how, customer loyalty, and other such economic intangibles, nor do these items meet the accounting definition of an asset because the company lacks unilateral control over them.

The current state of measurement technology does not allow for sufficiently reliable measurement of many intangibles. Information about them, therefore, is more appropriately addressed at Tier Two and Tier Three at this time.

DEFINING THE REPORTING ENTITY

This conceptual debate centers around which entities should be consolidated and under what criteria (including special purpose entities), how to account for joint ventures and other investments and alliances, and what kind of information should be conveyed in the financial statement footnotes. Resolving these issues requires agreement and convergence on some of the basic approaches to consolidation accounting, which currently vary between the United States and the rest of the world, as well as on the approach to segment reporting.

CONVERGENCE ISSUES

There are many important categories of standards in which significant differences exist between international standards and the major national standards, including those in the United States. The underlying differences have their roots deep in local customs, traditions, and business practices. Resolving the specific differences, however, will require that those involved reach some form of convergence of opinion or approach. The major categories of issues requiring convergence include:

- *Revenue recognition.* This involves the very basic but often complicated question of just when a revenue transaction is recognized and at what amount.

- *Liability and equity distinction.* The issue concerns drawing a line between the two and how to deal with compound instruments that have both liability and equity components.

- *Accounting for share-based payments.* Known in the United States as employee stock compensation, this has become a controversial issue because of the growing prevalence worldwide of this form of compensation, although in many parts of the world standards

Exhibit 2.2
Standard Setters and Market Regulators in the Corporate Reporting Supply Chain

| Company Executives | Boards of Directors | Independent Auditors | Information Distributors | Third-Party Analysts | Investors & Other Stakeholders |

Standard Setters

Market Regulators

Enabling Technologies

do not exist for these types of payments. These two factors have prompted the IASB to look at it more closely. While the IASB appears to be moving in the direction of expense recognition in relation to stock option awards, it is too soon to predict what its ultimate decision will be. In the United States, where this continues to be a subject of great debate, the FASB is closely monitoring the developments at the IASB. While, conceptually, expense treatment is the better answer, there are some very difficult measurement issues that would need to be resolved.

● *Existing standards in which the current approach is similar but rules differ.* These include accounting for pensions and for income taxes. The basic approach is the same among the major sets of standards. However, some of the specific rules differ, and this may lead, in some instances, to large differences in reported numbers.

Simply achieving convergence among standards will not result in common global reporting. A common approach to review and regulation will be necessary as well. Exhibit 2.2 illustrates the key roles played by standard setters and market regulators in the Corporate Reporting Supply Chain. Other requirements for achieving a true Global GAAP include common interpretation, high-quality auditing, and the requisite training and education for those who must apply and use the standards.

MOVING FROM VISION TO PRACTICE

Although it is part of a larger vision for a Three-Tier world, and in spite of the challenges mentioned earlier, Tier One has moved well beyond the visionary stage. Real progress has already been made toward developing a set of global accounting standards. This progress has come about through the efforts of the IASB under the leadership of its chairman, Sir David Tweedie, working with national standard setters across the world. Established in 2001 as the successor to the 30-year-old International Accounting Standards Committee, the IASB has as its mission to develop a set of accounting standards that can be used by companies all over the world. These standards are called International Financial Reporting Standards (IFRS).

The IASB's 14-member board includes liaisons who also work with the standard-setting bodies of Australia, Canada, France, Germany, Japan, New Zealand, the United Kingdom, and the United States. A variety of international organizations support the IASB's efforts, including the International Organization of Securities Commissions (IOSCO) and other key groups such as the European Commission and the Securities and Exchange Commission (SEC) in the United States.

The IASB does not have the power to force companies to use IFRS, either directly or indirectly. No global organization has this authority. Making these standards truly global will require the voluntary participation of countries, primarily each country's regulators. Absent other forces, if the gravitation toward the U.S. capital markets continues, the SEC will assume the global role by default.

EUROPEAN IMPETUS

The European Commission took a significant step toward global standards with the approval of the Financial Services Action Plan (May 1999), followed by the Lamfalussy Report on the Regulation of European Securities Markets (February 2001). This plan and report, endorsed by the European Parliament and approved at the highest levels of government in its member countries, call for an integrated capital market in order to provide greater liquidity for European companies at a lower cost of capital. The stated goal is to contribute to the development of "the most competitive and dynamic knowledge-based economy in the world."[12]

The plan calls for all listed companies in the European Union to report their financial results using International Financial Reporting Standards by 2005.[13] This applies to approximately 8,700 listed companies, representing about 25 percent of the world's total market capitalization. If the United States, with approximately 52 percent of the world's market capitalization, and Japan, accounting for another 9 percent,[14] were also to adopt these IFRS standards, they would for all practical purposes become global. Any other country that wanted to participate in the global economy would have virtually no choice but to use IFRS.

SECURING U.S. SUPPORT

Persuading the corporate reporting community in the United States to adopt IFRS will be a complicated task. Three broad models have been offered for accomplishing this. The so-called *convergence model,* the one embodied in the previously described IASB partnership with national standard setters, calls for merging U.S. GAAP, other major national standards, and IFRS to get "the best of all worlds." *The competitive model* would leave the decision to market forces by giving companies the option of using essentially either the IFRS or U.S. GAAP set of standards, and perhaps even a few others, within the exchanges on which they are listed.[15]

The third model could be termed *evolutionary,* combining features of the other two models and creating a situation where competition would lead to convergence over time as the different standard setters adopted the proven best practices. Whatever the approach is, the standards will necessarily be "market-tested" before they become institutionalized and supported globally.

This is not the place to debate which strategy can best achieve the goal of Global GAAP. The challenge now is to ensure that the United States remains engaged in the IASB's efforts, rather than becoming insular in its focus on domestic reform and legislative proposals that have arisen as a consequence of the Enron bankruptcy.

CREATING THE INTERPRETATIVE FUNCTION

Whether accounting standards are based on principles or rules, judgment is always exercised in their application. Every major national standard setter has a group that provides the official interpretation whenever unsatisfactory or conflicting interpretations develop or seem likely to develop.

The IASB's interpretative group, the International Financial Reporting Interpretation Committee (IFRIC) will need to work closely with its national counterparts (the U.K. Urgent Issues Task Force and the U.S. Emerging Issues Task Force, for example) in an effort to ensure that the process of standards convergence is not retarded or undermined by the emergence of differing national interpretations.

CREATING THE ENFORCEMENT FUNCTION

With interpretation must come enforcement. The traditions of regulatory enforcement of accounting standards are quite different around the world. The SEC, as market regulator, carries out this function in the United States. In the United Kingdom, enforcement is delegated by government to an independent panel. A number of major economies are still considering how enforcement should be effected. The common theme, however, is that the regulatory group typically stands apart from the group that sets the standards.

Creating an enforcement function for Global GAAP will be challenging and will require the national enforcement groups to find solutions. The challenge of enforcement differs from standard setting in one important respect. While one body may ultimately set standards "for the world," each country will need its own regulatory function with access to local juridical process to pursue offenders.

One possible solution may be the creation of a body called, for lack of a better term, the International Financial Reporting Enforcement Committee (IFREC), which would not itself take regulatory action but would seek to facilitate the common interpretation of accounting standards by the national regulatory functions. Consistent with today's national structures, however, this enforcement body would be distinct from both standard setting (IASB) and standard interpretation (IFRIC).

THE FUTURE IS A JOURNEY

One final challenge remains: Standards must keep pace with the world as it changes. Once the world gets to Global GAAP, the work has only just begun. Over time, the principles on which Global GAAP is based could devolve into rules. Inevitably, guidelines would be issued as clarification and interpretation are sought. An essential adjunct to Global GAAP is a commitment on the part of all (and a process to ensure respect for the commitment) to continuously review standards and interpretations as they develop. Standards that no longer serve their purpose should be discarded or replaced by better standards based on better principles. Pruning and reseeding will be necessary to ensure that Global GAAP endures.

NOTES

1. Based on the aggregate results as of April 2002 from the ongoing PricewaterhouseCoopers industry surveys. See Value-Reporting Web site, www.valuereporting.com. Very similar results for investors and analysts were obtained from PricewaterhouseCoopers' 14 country surveys conducted in 1997 and 1998.

2. Nanette Byrnes, David Henry, and Mike McNamee, "Confused about earnings? You're not alone. Here's what companies

should do—and what investors need to know," *BusinessWeek,* November 26, 2001, 76ff.

3. Ibid.

4. Baruch Lev and Paul Zarowin, *The Boundaries of Financial Reporting and How to Extend Them* (Paris, France: Organization for Economic Co-Operation and Development, 1998), 17.

5. For a discussion of the uses and limitations of price/earnings (P/E) ratios, see Robert G. Eccles, *The ValueReporting Revolution,* Chapter 2.

6. See Eccles, *The ValueReporting Revolution,* 56.

7. Source for the Standard & Poor's market to book ratio statistics: Morningstar Principia Pro.

8. For a detailed discussion of The Earnings Game see Eccles, *The ValueReporting Revolution,* Chapter 4.

9. "Security returns clearly incorporate a large set of information beyond earnings surprise, because earnings surprise information explains only a small fraction of the overall variation in returns." (William Kinney, David Burgstahler, and Roger Martin, "The Materiality of Earnings Surprise," working paper, University of Texas at Austin, University of Washington, Seattle, and Kelly School of Business, Indiana University, Bloomington, July 8, 1999, 24–25.) Other studies have shown that companies that consistently beat expectations across a certain threshold actually do worse than a comparable peer group. Francois Degeorge, Jayendu Patel, and Richard Zeckhauser, "Earnings Management to Exceed Thresholds," *Journal of Business,* January 1999, Vol. 72, No.1.

10. Data source: WhisperNumber.com, www.whispernumbers. com.

11. Francesco Guerrera, "Bolkestein: breath of fresh air or maverick?" *Financial Times,* February 20, 2002. Also see news.ft.com/ft/gx.cgi/ftc?pagename=View&c=Article&cid= FT378KCLXXC&live=true.

12. Frits Bolkestein, "The Lisbon European Council: A new stimulus towards the integration of European financial markets," speech in Forum Financier Belge, Brussels, May 4, 2000. Also see europa.eu.int/comm/internal_market/en/speeches/spch163.htm.

13. Companies already using U.S. GAAP as their primary basis of accounting have until 2007 to convert, as do companies that only have publicly traded debt.

14. Source: World Federation of Exchanges, www.world-exchanges.org. Data cited were as of February 2002 and include only the major stock exchanges in the European Union member countries, the United States, and Japan.

15. Sunder Shyam, "Standards for Corporate Financial Reporting: Regulatory Competition Within and Across Boundaries," working paper, Yale School of Management, Yale University, April 2002.

CHAPTER THREE

---◆---

INDUSTRY STANDARDS

The objectives of transparency, accountability, and integrity will not be fulfilled if the reporting model fails to move beyond the establishment and adoption of Tier-One Global GAAP. A fundamental set of financial measures at Tier One will provide general comparability among companies in all industries everywhere and getting this far will be an outstanding achievement. But investors and stakeholders also need more complete, reliable, and useful information on a company's overall performance and prospects within its own industry—Tier-Two supplementary financial and nonfinancial information. This information is not readily available within today's corporate reporting model driven by GAAP.

Certain companies already report a small amount of this information. In the post-Enron era, companies rush to make ever more information available, but more reams of paper and CD-ROMs packed with data will not solve the problem. The problem is twofold:

1. Identifying the key value drivers in an industry and developing standardized measures for them, and

2. Achieving global comparability in how companies report on these measures across a given industry.

In today's global economy, companies compete in global industries, and both companies and their stakeholders want and need to compare corporate performance among competitors, regardless of national origin. How do Spanish banks compare to Swiss banks, U.K. pharmaceutical companies to U.S. pharmaceutical companies, German automakers to their Japanese counterparts?

THE CASE FOR TIER-TWO STANDARDS

The case for Tier-Two standards is straightforward:

- GAAP-based financial statements are important, but they do not cover all of the value drivers, many of which are nonfinancial in nature.

- The complete set of value drivers differs significantly across industries.

- Different industries often define and measure the same value driver differently.

- Most important, different *companies* within a single industry often define and measure the same value driver differently.

For investors and stakeholders to make well-informed decisions about companies, they need information of this kind.

If they need truly *relevant* information in these areas, relevance implies industry-specific measures. If they need truly *comparable* information, comparability implies commonly accepted definitions of measures and commonly accepted metrics. If "commonly accepted" is the watchword here, then standards are the solution. These standards are the basis of Tier Two in the Three-Tier Model of Corporate Transparency (Exhibit 3.1).

More standards may sound like a bad idea, but those who doubt the need for them have only to listen more closely to what is happening in the world around them. Investors, analysts, and stakeholders are demanding more information.

Exhibit 3.1
Tier Two in the Three-Tier Model of
Corporate Transparency

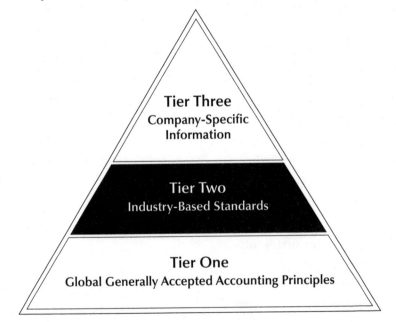

Standards for Tier-Two information are already emerging in some industries and some countries. Even traditional standard setters and regulatory bodies are recognizing the need for more information and encouraging companies to report more richly.

What should Tier-Two standards be? Who should develop them? Who, if anyone, should be charged with enforcing them? The simple answer is: Tier-Two standards should be developed by industry participants themselves, and they should be voluntary, not regulated. In addition to companies themselves, other members of the Corporate Reporting Supply Chain need to be involved as well: accounting firms, analysts, and investors. As these Tier-Two standards are developed, new *de facto* standard setters will join the supply chain as well and may end up getting the support of market regulators (Exhibit 3.2). One of the facts of corporate life, however, is that if industries do not take the initiative to develop these standards, someone else will do so to meet the market demand.

An example that indicates the interest in industry-specific reporting is growing: In 2001 the U.S. Financial Accounting Standards Board (FASB) published the results of a broad study to determine the kinds of business information

Exhibit 3.2
The Corporate Reporting Supply Chain and Tier-Two Standards Development

that companies in eight selected industries report in addition to their financial statements.[1] The stated objective of the report, *Improving Business Reporting: Insights into Enhancing Voluntary Disclosures,* was to help companies improve their business reporting, "by providing evidence that many leading companies are making extensive voluntary disclosures."[2] The report also provides many real-life examples of such voluntary disclosures, which can serve as "helpful ideas" for others on how to describe and explain a company's investment potential.

The findings and recommendations in the study included the following:

- Many leading companies are voluntarily disclosing extensive business information that appears to be useful in communicating effectively to investors.

- The importance of voluntary disclosures is expected to increase in the future because of the fast pace of change in the business environment.

- Voluntary disclosures should cover not only good news but also disappointments.

- Disclosures are most useful if they report on previously announced plans, goals, and results achieved in pursuing those plans and goals.

- Companies are encouraged to continue improving their business reporting while experimenting with the types of information disclosed and the manner of its disclosure.[3]

In many respects, the report makes a convincing case for transparency, with concepts and research findings that apply worldwide. The FASB report, together with examples in this chapter of worldwide initiatives to develop Tier-Two-related guidelines and standards, should be persuasive enough. Taken as a whole, they tell industries that clearly defined and consistently used industry-specific standards are needed and that the opportunity exists to take the lead in developing them through industry-wide collaboration. They counsel corporate executives to disclose voluntarily the information that stakeholders legitimately want and need. They argue that just as Tier-Two information is important to corporate executives as a practical management tool, it is also important to stakeholders, who have in general become much more sophisticated and demanding users of corporate information. Industry-specific standards will create a broad commonality in reporting among peer companies—hence transparency and order, not confusion.

A TALE OF TWO INDUSTRIES

A brief comparison of two large and highly visible industries, pharmaceuticals and telecommunications, demonstrates the logic of developing industry-specific Tier-Two standards. The point of this example is to show distinct and significant differences between the two industries to underscore the importance of complete, high-quality, industry-specific information. Such information obviously has an internal role—managing the company well and creating shareholder value. It has a role in communications—reporting on performance. In addition, it has a role in investment decisions.

Consider, for example, the product development cycle. Before a new drug can come to market, it must undergo excruciatingly detailed regulatory scrutiny. This makes product development a very long and costly process. In addition,

government regulations dictate how products can be manu-
factured, marketed, sold, and delivered. This makes the
market very difficult for new entrants. In the telecommunications industry, on the other hand, deregulation and pri-
vatization have totally changed the industry's market
dynamics. Although regulation still sets the rules of the
game concerning competition and collaboration among industry players, many new competitors have entered the service provider marketplace, including TV cable companies
offering telephone and high-speed Internet access services.

Innovation is the heart of the value creation strategy in
pharmaceutical companies (i.e., creating new drugs and di-
agnostics targeted to specific diseases). The importance of
the intellectual capital and other intangible assets in this
industry is reflected in its market to book ratio of 7.4 in
April 2002.[4] Profit margins on successful pharmaceutical
products can be large, due to the high level of risk involved
in developing them, and products are protected by patents
that extend for many years. Once products have been developed and approved—this is the very costly part of the business—the manufacturing process is relatively inexpensive,
although closely scrutinized by regulators (e.g., the Food
and Drug Administration in the United States).

In the telecommunications industry, on the other hand,
the innovation dynamic is very different. Wireline network
service providers, for example, invested large sums in fiber
optics a few years ago, but a new technology emerged that
increased capacity about eight-fold. As a result, these service providers now have enormous overcapacity. Their service offering has become little more than a commodity, and
their market strategies focus on attracting and retaining
large numbers of customers, competing on price, and introducing new products and services very quickly.

Because innovation is of such strategic importance for pharmaceutical companies, research and development is the key to value creation, and intellectual capital is arguably the most valuable asset in the industry. That asset may now be at risk in some respects. Government intervention in drug pricing and action in the wake of the 2001 anthrax scare in the United States have both challenged the historically sacrosanct patent rights that pharmaceutical companies have enjoyed.

In the telecommunications industry, intellectual capital is of lesser importance than effective marketing strategies, brand development, customer satisfaction and retention, and ensuring that appropriate network capacity is in place. New products proliferate quickly, although many are simply product extensions on a basic service, such as voicemail or call waiting, and there is a high rate of new product failure.

Until a few years ago, financial performance differed significantly between the industries. In the pharmaceutical world, the relatively slower pace of product development and healthy profit margins meant that reported earnings of the large companies were more predictable from quarter to quarter. Successful products that generated revenues and profits for many years resulted in moderate price/earnings (P/E) ratios. Not surprisingly, the volatility of these stocks, as measured by their beta,[5] was fairly low at 0.41.[6] Strong cash flows, high returns on equity, and a strong capital base resulted in a very conservative debt to equity ratio of 0.26.[7]

This does not describe the telecommunications world. New technologies, an industry structure now fracturing more than consolidating, and unproven business models among some of the new entrants have led to a chaotic capital market environment for telecommunications. The industry beta is fairly high (1.31 for wireline providers and 1.59

for wireless providers),[8] the trend in stock prices has been largely down in the past few years (dramatically so in some subsectors) and debt to equity ratios (0.63 for wireline and 0.92 for wireless)[9] have soared, as have bankruptcies. The P/E multiples for wireline and wireless cannot be calculated for the industry as a whole because earnings are non-existent. The current market to book ratio for the wireless sector is 4.9,[10] reasonably close to that of the Standard & Poor's 500, which is 4.3, as mentioned in Chapter 2. For the wireline sector, the market to book ratio is actually 0.9,[11] which means that market value is actually *less* than book value—a telling commentary by the market.

IMPLICATIONS FOR VALUE DRIVERS

Given the differences between these two industries, important differences in strategies for value creation would be expected. Surveys conducted by PricewaterhouseCoopers with executives, analysts, and institutional investors show that this is indeed true.[12] Exhibit 3.3 reports the performance measures that executives in each industry rated highly important in making internal decisions. They chose these measures from a much longer list developed by industry experts. That the longer, industry-specific lists of performance measures were very different for each industry reinforces the argument for Tier-Two standards. Please note that the value drivers listed in Exhibit 3.3 are not ranked according to the participating executives' perceptions of their relative importance. They are simply organized by category for ease of comparison.

Earnings, a measure defined in all forms of GAAP, made both lists. This is not surprising. However, even a cursory glance at the table reveals that *many of the most important*

Exhibit 3.3
Key Value Drivers for Executives in the Pharmaceutical and Telecommunications Industries

Pharmaceuticals	Telecommunications
Earnings	Earnings
Performance by business segment	Cash flow by business segment
Market growth and potential by therapeutic area	Revenue metrics by driver
Market growth and potential by geographic area	Significant operating costs by category
Market share by therapeutic area	Capital expenditures
R&D pipeline	Competitive landscape
Product focus strategy	Market growth
Product innovation strategy	Network reach, quality, and capability
Effectiveness of product launch	Pricing strategy
Reputation with prescribers	Sales and marketing strategy
Regulatory issues	Customer churn rate
Quality of management	Regulatory environment

value drivers are not covered by GAAP, nor are they subject to any standardized measurement or reporting. Further, the two lists of value drivers differ very considerably, indicating that different standards for each industry are required.

In the pharmaceuticals column, three of the most important value drivers relate to the market for products, three relate to the products themselves, and another relates to the R&D pipeline that makes products possible. In contrast, telecommunications focuses more on customers through its network capabilities, pricing strategy, sales and marketing strategy, and customer churn rate. In both industries, the majority of the most important value drivers connect to differing features of their industries, and the majority are not addressed by any form of GAAP.

DEVELOPING INDUSTRY-SPECIFIC STANDARDS: THREE EXAMPLES

The comparison just drawn makes the case that different industries need industry-specific standards. Yet the concept of Tier-Two industry-based standards is probably enough to send every participant in the Corporate Reporting Supply Chain running for cover—save for investors, deeply involved stakeholders, and perhaps a few analysts. The concept is new and untested. This reality makes the development of Tier-Two standards an even greater challenge.

Few, if any, industries or organizations have acquired enough practical experience to offer definitive guidance. Further, it seems clear that for the development effort to generate robust standards, the effort must be highly collaborative. A concerted effort will also be required to ensure that the resulting standards are credible in the eyes of those who adhere to them as a framework for reporting, those who provide assurance on them, and those who use information gathered and formatted under their guidance.

Collaboration. The very word collaboration raises a red flag, as collaborative efforts are reputed to take on a very long life of their own. Because the current need is so great, industries must find a way to create standards and implement them without decades of work. Evidence is mounting of the will to develop the kinds of standards that Tier Two requires, and a few current initiatives offer insight as to how this can be accomplished.

BUSINESS LEADERSHIP: THE PRO FORMA EXAMPLE

The struggle to use a single set of standards for measuring earnings across and within industries has erupted into a growing and acrimonious debate about pro forma earnings, especially in the United States. Pro forma earnings are calculated differently from GAAP earnings. They exclude certain "special" or "one-time" charges (and even revenues) that are considered "nonrecurring," such as investment gains and losses or restructuring charges. The theory holds that by excluding these charges the reported earnings are supposedly more "sustainable," in that they are free from one-time items. However, there are usually many one-time items that differ across accounting periods, and periods without such items are really the exception. Comparability can be hampered if different items are in-/excluded over periods.

The use of pro forma earnings varies by industry. A manufacturing company that does not make many acquisitions or rely on complex financial instruments to hedge currency risks has a relatively easy task of measuring revenues and costs and determining the period in which both occur. On the other hand, a high-technology company might have a history of many acquisitions and a growing percentage of revenues derived from service contracts on which revenues are earned over a period of years. Such a company would find calculating earnings to be a much more complex task than would the manufacturing company.

The critics of pro forma complain that the measure is poorly defined, pointing out that even the name for it varies widely: "operating earnings," "core earnings," "ongoing earnings," and "economic earnings." Critics also charge that this is just one more example of The Earnings Game. A May 14, 2001, cover article in *BusinessWeek* summed up this view in no uncertain terms: "Companies use every trick to pump earnings and fool investors. The latest abuse, 'Pro forma' reporting."[13]

Those who object to the use of pro forma earnings may also see it as way for management to boost earnings and deflate P/E ratios artificially, so that the company's stock appears to be reasonably priced. When companies rush at the end of a reporting quarter to announce pro forma earnings—which are not covered by formal accounting standards and not audited—detractors see this as a way to capture investor attention before GAAP earnings are reported and formally filed several weeks later. When GAAP earnings finally become publicly available, they are barely noticed. The market has already accepted the pro forma numbers as that quarter's earnings. Further, that quarter's earnings are by then ancient history, and all players are already anticipating next quarter's earnings report.

However, pro forma has its defenders. They argue that they are forthrightly trying to give analysts and investors the most realistic picture of a company's underlying performance. To do so, they must separate out the effects of unusual items and compensate for elements of GAAP accounting, which, in their view, are actually misleading. "The pro forma numbers are how we think about our business, and how Wall Street analysts follow it," Amazon spokesman Bill Curry was quoted as saying in the *BusinessWeek* cover story. He emphasized, however, that his company reports GAAP numbers along with pro forma numbers.[14]

Other proponents argue that pro forma is simply better than GAAP earnings as a measure of the predictability of the bottom line. There is survey evidence that the market finds pro forma earnings a useful measure. A survey conducted by Broadgate Consultants, Inc. about some recent Financial Accounting Standards Board initiatives found that of the 223 fund managers surveyed, about three-fourths of them consider pro forma earnings either somewhat useful or extremely useful, and approximately two-thirds oppose banning pro forma reporting.[15]

Reforming pro forma

Resolving the controversy that surrounds pro forma requires agreement on precisely what pro forma means and how it should be reported, while recognizing that pro forma earnings belong in the context of other value-relevant information. In most circumstances when companies report pro forma earnings, information users are justified in assuming that management is trying to do the right thing by providing more meaningful information and not, as critics assert, simply painting a rosier performance picture. However, the critics cannot be faulted for arguing that this information is of limited utility because it cannot be compared across periods for a company, across business segments within a company, and across companies within an industry. The survey by Broadgate Consultants found that a remarkable 95 percent of money managers would like more consistency in the reporting of pro forma earnings.[16] The leap from that view to a push for standardized pro forma reporting is not too great.

Modeling in advance how Tier-Two standards could develop, the business community has already stepped forward to voice concerns about the consistency and comparability of pro forma earnings. Standard & Poor's has attempted to create a lexicon by distinguishing among "as reported earnings," "operating earnings," and "pro forma earnings," and has suggested the circumstances in which each is most appropriately used.[17] Standard & Poor's has also offered clear definitions for the first two. On pro forma earnings, the company proposed the rigorous view that "this concept should be used only in special cases where the impact of a possible change, such as a merger, is being considered."[18] As part of its effort to bring consistency to the measurement of earnings for use in analysis, Standard & Poor's has also proposed a definition of "core earnings" that refers to "the after-tax earnings generated from a corporation's principal business or businesses."[19] Core earnings "focus on a company's ongoing operations" and are calculated by making some well-defined adjustments to reported earnings.[20]

Two professional associations, Financial Executives International (FEI) and the National Investor Relations Institute (NIRI), have jointly suggested an approach to reporting pro forma earnings.[21] In a press release termed "a cautionary note," the organizations wrote that if earnings are communicated on a pro forma basis—i.e., on a basis other than GAAP—then reconciliation of those earnings to GAAP should be provided. It went on to state that the information should be presented with a balanced perspective, acknowledging, however, that management does not have an arm's-length view.

The U.S. Securities and Exchange Commission (SEC), in a noteworthy move, has validated the cautionary counsel of the FEI and NIRI. This suggests that solutions devised by and for the business community can gain legitimacy. The SEC first approvingly cited this effort in a cautionary release of its own, "to sound a warning to public companies and other registrants who present to the public their earnings and results of operations on the basis of methodologies other than Generally Accepted Accounting Principles . . . ."[22] In that release, the SEC encouraged public companies to "consider and follow" the FEI/NIRI recommendations. In doing so, the SEC said that a presentation of financial results "that sets forth calculations of financial results on a basis other than GAAP generally will not be deemed to be misleading merely due to its deviation from GAAP if the company in the same public statement discloses in plain English how it has deviated from GAAP and the amounts of those deviations."[23]

What the SEC appears to be saying is that companies should follow these guidelines, or else they could face consequences. The SEC communication is not regulation. It is, however, a message to the corporate reporting world: If you do not follow the FEI/NIRI guidelines, you are on your own. The real-world impact of the SEC's statements will probably be much the same as if the Commission had issued and enforced a regulatory rule, and there is merit in continuing to move forward on this issue.

A logical middle ground can be found between the highly restrictive guidelines proposed by Standard & Poor's and the cautionary guidelines introduced by the FEI and NIRI and reinforced by the SEC. This middle ground is to develop standards for reporting pro forma earnings along industry lines, since companies report pro forma earnings for reasons that vary widely by industry. John Chambers, president and CEO of Cisco, has suggested that the FEI/NIRI recommendations be taken as the starting point for a minimal set of pro forma criteria. He also acknowledged that real benefits for investors, analysts, and companies could be obtained if individual industry groups developed their own more refined set of standards.[24]

The FEI/NIRI guidelines on pro forma reporting provide a clue to how Tier-Two standards could be developed by collaboration across industry-specific professional or functional groups. Two other ongoing initiatives to create reporting guidelines outside the traditional financial realm also provide insight. The first is an initiative of the Danish Agency for Trade and Industry to develop guidelines for intellectual capital statements. The second is the Global Reporting Initiative (GRI) to develop sustainability reporting guidelines on economic, environmental, and social performance. Although neither of these initiatives is industry-based, and both could eventually compete with an industry-based approach to Tier Two, they provide useful insights into how to develop standards outside the purview of the more traditional accounting standard-setting processes. Each is worth a closer look.

GOVERNMENT/CORPORATE COLLABORATION: A DANISH INITIATIVE

In November 2000, the Danish Agency for Trade and Industry (www.efs.dk) issued an interesting publication: *A Guideline for Intellectual Capital Statements.* Its purpose was "to find new ways of creating values, both tangible and intangible, in all processes of our society, based on the development, sharing and application of knowledge."[25] In this publication, the Agency develops the idea that guidelines for intellectual capital statements can improve both internal and public reporting as well as knowledge management within companies. Naturally, the Agency expects improved external reporting to give stakeholders a better grasp of the reporting company's knowledge management. With legitimate satisfaction, the Agency states that it has "taken the international lead in being the first country to develop a guideline for preparing intellectual capital statements, *based on the concrete experience of 17 companies* [emphasis added]."[26]

These guidelines were not created in a laboratory test tube. Instead, the Agency solicited the voluntary participation of companies and arranged for them to be supported by input from academic researchers, industrial organizations, consultants, and government officials. The innovation and experience of the 17 companies led directly to the published guidelines.

The report acknowledges that while it "does not provide ultimate answers,"[27] it offers metrics for a variety of "indicators" of intellectual capital, such as customer satisfaction with staff, competency and career planning, internal knowledge and knowledge sharing, patent claims, product innovation rate, and ratio of new products to total turnover. These indicators are similar to some of the nonfinancial value drivers cited above from the pharmaceutical and telecommunications industry surveys. Although the suggested metrics are not proposed standards in the full sense—they are not advanced as the sole and proper way to measure these "indicators"—they are only one step away from being such.

INTERNATIONAL COLLABORATION: THE GLOBAL REPORTING INITIATIVE

The Global Reporting Initiative (GRI) (www.globalreporting.org), begun in 1997 by the Coalition for Environmentally Responsible Economies in partnership with the United Nations Environment Programme, explicitly defines its mission as developing "reporting guidelines for voluntary use by organizations reporting on the economic, environmental, and social dimensions of their activities, products, and services."[28]

In its year 2000 *Sustainability Reporting Guidelines,* the GRI wrote that "nonfinancial reporting to date has not been guided by a widely accepted, common framework of principles and practices as to what should be reported or how, when and where."[29] In its draft 2002 document by the same name, the GRI describes its long-term objective of developing "generally accepted sustainability accounting principles."[30] Notably, in a discussion of "sector supplements" in the draft for 2002, the GRI states that it "recognizes the limits of a one-size-fits-all approach and the importance of capturing the unique set of sustainability issues faced by different industry sectors."[31] To address this need, the GRI is already at work on supplemental industry-specific rules.

The GRI's recognition that one size does not fit all is remarkably similar to the assertion in the Three-Tier Model of Corporate Transparency that complete assessment of corporate performance requires industry-specific measures. Other parallels between the GRI guidelines and the call for transparency in this book are unmistakable: consistency, accuracy, timeliness, and auditability. Further, the GRI's process for developing both core and sector standards might very well serve as a model, or at least a strong start, for the development of Tier-Two standards. The GRI's process is collaborative and inclusive of companies, environmental and social NGOs, accounting organizations, employees, investors, and other stakeholders worldwide. Its efforts are to be guided by a steering committee with representatives from all of these groups.[32]

Are companies paying attention? According to a press release by GRI on its April 2002 meeting in New York, "more than 110 pioneering companies from around the world have already undertaken sustainability reporting using the GRI Guidelines—including BASF, British Telecom, Bristol-Myers Squibb, Canon, Co-operative Bank, Danone, Electrolux, Ford, GM, Interface, KLM, NEC, Nike, Novo Group, Nokia, Shell, and South African Breweries."[33] The news release also quotes Allen White, acting chief executive of the GRI, as saying, "The GRI represents a turning point in expanding corporate disclosure with critical information that complements financial statements. We believe this is a major step toward strengthening capital markets and enriching information flows to investors, advocacy groups, labor and other interested parties."[34]

Does the GRI provide a good model for developing Tier-Two standards? Perhaps, perhaps not. What the GRI does demonstrate, however, is that when stakeholders demand information, governments and companies will listen and respond. It demonstrates that collaboration and initiative can produce results that many might not expect in the face of sometimes-controversial issues. And it shows that the process can move quickly. In the space of five years, the GRI has moved beyond developing core guidelines to working on supplemental guidelines for specific industries. Even if some more refined model ultimately surpasses the GRI model, the Corporate Reporting Supply Chain can learn valuable lessons from the GRI's experience.

AN EMERGING MODEL FOR TIER-TWO STANDARD-SETTING

Disparate as the three initiatives just discussed may be—reporting pro forma earnings in the United States; reporting on intellectual capital in Denmark; and GRI reporting on economic, social, and environmental performance—they share some common characteristics. They all begin with innovations introduced into practice by individual companies. They all learn from these efforts to identify the most effective ways of measuring and reporting, and they all codify this knowledge into a set of guidelines or standards. They all involve broad constituencies in developing guidelines or standards. They all rely on voluntary reporting according to the guidelines, and they all permit some form of independent verification. There are lessons learned here that can help to guide the development and application of industry-based Tier-Two standards.

Developing these standards will not be easy and difficult questions remain, including:

- How difficult and costly will it be for companies to develop the internal systems and processes required to report according to the new standards?

- Who will determine what groups are qualified to provide assurance, and how will the assurance provider do so?

- What are the legal risks to standard setters, companies, and assurance providers, and how will these risks be managed?

- How will investors and stakeholders learn to make the best use of this new information?

- Should Tier-Two standards become mandatory? If so, when?

- What technologies are required to make more complete, higher quality, and more usable information available to all?

Truly visionary companies—both those that foresee the competitive advantage in this process as well as those that simply want to do the right thing—will pioneer the use of Tier-Two standards and reporting. A few pioneers, however, can create a land rush. If the standards are sound, all stakeholders will find them valuable and will exert pressure on other companies to report on that basis. The pressure will be applied either directly (by demanding the information) or indirectly (by not investing in the companies' stocks, not buying their products, protesting their labor practices, and so on).

The sound new practices will begin to prevail. The leadership of a few companies will eventually gather up other companies in an industry. There will be diehards, of course—companies that refuse to report according to Tier-Two standards or to report any Tier-Two information at all—but economic forces and the consequences of lost public trust will separate the winners from the rest.

Just as companies need to experiment with how to measure and report on non-GAAP value drivers, so do industry-based groups need to experiment with how standards should be developed. Just as a few pioneering companies in an industry can set the example for others, a few pioneering industries can lay the foundation for developing Tier-Two standards across many other industries. In the same time frame that Global GAAP is being developed, a critical mass of industries will be needed to do the same for Tier-Two standards.

The time to start is now, and public trust depends on it. This is not merely a book about companies and industries and their patterns of reporting. It is a book about building public trust in companies and industries. Here Tier-Two standards are crucial.

NOTES

1. Business Reporting Research Project: *Improving Business Reporting: Insights into Enhancing Voluntary Disclosures*, Steering Committee Report Series (Federal Accounting Standards Board, 2001).

2. Ibid., v.

3. Ibid., v–vi.

4. Source: Dow Jones Interactive, April 2002.

5. Atomica.com defines beta as "A mathematical measure of the sensitivity of rates of return on a portfolio or a given stock compared with rates of return on the market as a whole. A high beta (greater than 1.0) indicates moderate or high price volatility. A beta of 1.5 forecasts a 1.5% change in the return on an asset for every 1% in the return on the market. High-beta stocks are best to own in a strong bull market but are worst to own in a bear market."

6. Source: Dow Jones Interactive, April 2002.

7. Ibid.

8. Ibid.

9. Ibid.

10. Ibid.

11. Ibid.

12. See ValueReporting Web site, www.valuereporting.com.

13. David Henry, "The Numbers Game," *BusinessWeek*, May 14, 2001, 100–110.

14. Ibid.

15. PR Newswire, "Three Fourths of Portfolio Managers Surveyed Find Pro Forma Reporting Useful," press release, (New York: PR Newswire), November 7, 2001. Also see www.prnewswire.com/cgi-bin/stories.pl?ACCT=105&STORY=/www/story/11-07-2001/0001610493.

16. Ibid.

17. David M. Blitzer, Robert E. Friedman, and Howard J. Silverblatt, "Standard & Poor's Position on Operating Earnings," Standard & Poor's, November 16, 2001. Also see www.compustat. com/www/press/operatingearnings.html.

18. Ibid.

19. David M. Blitzer, Robert E. Friedman, and Howard J. Silverblatt, "Measures of Corporate Earnings," Standard & Poor's, May 14, 2002, 4. Also see www.spglobal.com/earnings_press.html.

20. Ibid., 4–5.

21. Louis M. Thompson, Jr. "NIRI Releases Survey: An Analysis of Corporate Use of Pro Forma Reporting," *The National Investor Relations Institutes Executive Alerts,* January 17, 2002. Also see www.niri.org/publications/alerts/ea20020117.cfm.

22. U.S. Securities and Exchange Commission, "Cautionary Advice Regarding the Use of 'Pro Forma' Financial Information in Earnings Releases," Other Commission Orders, Notices, and Information, Release Nos.: 33-8039, 34-45124, FR-59, (New York: U.S. Securities and Exchange Commission, December 4, 2001).

23. Ibid.

24. Eccles interview: John Chambers, president and CEO of Cisco, February 19, 2002.

25. Danish Agency for Trade and Industry, Ministry of Trade and Industry, *A Guideline for Intellectual Capital Statements: A Key to Knowledge Management* (Copenhagen, Denmark: Danish Agency for Trade and Industry, Ministry of Trade and Industry, November 2000). Also see www.efs.dk/publikationer/rapporter/ guidelineics/ren.htm.

26. Ibid.

27. Ibid.

28. *2000 Sustainability Reporting Guidelines on Economic, Environmental, and Social Performance,* Global Reporting Initiative, 1.

29. Ibid., 2.

30. *2002 Sustainability Reporting Guidelines (draft),* Global Reporting Initiative, April 1, 2002, 9. Also see www.globalreporting.org/GRIGuidelines/index.htm.

31. Ibid., 12.

32. *2000 Sustainability Reporting Guidelines on Economic, Environmental, and Social Performance,* Global Reporting Initiative.

33. "Global Reporting Initiative Inaugurated at U.N. Event: A Milestone for Corporate Disclosure and Transparency," press release (New York: Global Reporting Initiative), April 4, 2002. Also see www.globalreporting.org/News/PR/Inauguration04-04-02.htm.

34. Ibid.

CHAPTER FOUR

GOOD MANAGEMENT

In today's world of celebrity CEOs, good management is often taken to mean personal and highly visible leadership and little else. For those who stay in touch with the latest thinking about management practice, good management is also likely to mean the application in business of complex new ideas, often glossed by an acronym such as JIT or CRM. No one can seriously doubt that able leadership is needed, or that new strategic and operational concepts can make a huge difference. But there is another meaning to good management: identifying, measuring, using internally, and reporting externally on the *real value drivers* of a company.

This sounds as if it is all in a day's work, part of normal practice in every well-managed company. In reality, companies are so complex today that management can easily underestimate the importance of certain value drivers or simply fail to give them any importance at all. As this chapter should make clear, contemporary thinking about what drives value in a company needs a good airing, and there are strong new views that deserve close attention.

Internal information about the real value drivers of a company serves as the basis both for effective management and for appropriately transparent external reporting. The real value drivers range from measures at Tier One and Tier Two to measures—both financial and nonfinancial—at Tier Three. These Tier–Three measures may well include information about strategy, identified risks, risk management and compliance, compensation policies, corporate governance, and company-specific performance measures on key value drivers. To report publicly and completely on these value drivers, within the bounds of competitive good sense, is the very meaning of transparency.

Exhibit 4.1
Tier Three in the Three-Tier Model of Corporate Transparency

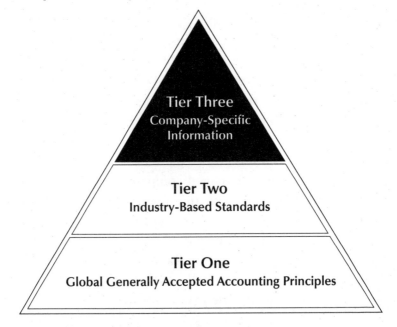

Tier Three
Company-Specific Information

Tier Two
Industry-Based Standards

Tier One
Global Generally Accepted Accounting Principles

Management turns its commitment to transparency into action by making its holistic value proposition understandable to stakeholders. *Holistic* here means how all things within the company, and between the company and its markets, are linked. By demonstrating to stakeholders the links between marketplace opportunities and strategy, between value drivers and measured results, and between management decisions and value creation, the company will deserve the confidence of investors and all stakeholders in its performance. Good management and good reporting at Tier Three (Exhibit 4.1) produces good results at Tier One and Tier Two.

MEASUREMENT MATTERS

A truism: Management should measure and manage those things that create value and help the company to meet the legitimate expectations of its stakeholders. In practice, this elementary advice can be difficult to follow across the full complexity of a company. Doing so requires clear articulation of a company's strategy at both the corporate and business unit levels. It also requires identifying the value drivers that must be measured and managed. The concept of value drivers is still fresh; it remains compelling and challenging. Not too long ago, companies measured and managed almost exclusively by the numbers—the financial ones.

Financial results still matter enormously. But as this chapter will demonstrate, companies have both financial and nonfinancial variables of critical importance. Together they make the company what it is and generate its future. Today there is an increasing commitment among senior executives to recognize and manage a fuller range of key variables—the real value drivers. A major theme of this book bears just on this point: Companies should also report on these real value drivers publicly and rigorously.

Measurement plays a dual role: it focuses attention on what is important, as determined by the company's strategy, and it monitors the level of performance along those dimensions in the effort to turn strategy into results. Although measurement is inherently based on information about events that have already happened, certain measures can be predictive in nature when the relationships among value drivers are well understood. If management has identified its key value drivers and developed reliable means of measuring them, effective use of those measures as a management tool will inevitably create value for shareholders and other stakeholders (or more effectively preserve value in difficult times).

WHAT CREATES VALUE?

What does management consider to be the real value drivers? A PricewaterhouseCoopers Management Barometer Survey conducted in third-quarter 2001 queried 157 U.S. executives in a number of industries about several broad categories of value drivers.[1] Some key research results appear in Exhibit 4.2.[2]

The executives considered *product and service quality, customer satisfaction and loyalty,* and *operational efficiency* to be more important value drivers than *current accounting results.* Consistent with this finding, the executives also gave high priority to these three nonfinancial value drivers as determinants of future financial results, and a large majority reported that they consider these three value drivers in making internal decisions. The same is true for *product and*

Exhibit 4.2
Executive Perceptions of Eight Value Drivers*

Value-driver category	Important for creating shareholder value over the long term	Has a high impact on future financial performance	Use the measure in evaluation and decision making
Product and service quality	89	86	83
Customer satisfaction and loyalty	83	86	73
Operational efficiency	75	75	72
Current accounting results	71	62	81
Product and service innovation	62	60	54
Employee satisfaction and turnover	47	44	38
Alliances with other companies	20	22	17
Community involvement and environmental performance	11	8	11

Note: The left-hand column lists the categories of value drivers tested, while the statements across the top of the chart reflect how executives perceive or use each value driver. The figures record percentage of executives who agreed with the statements.

* All percentages evaluated on a five-point scale, with 5 the highest and 1 the lowest rating. Percentages are based on respondents who responded with a 5 or 4 to the questions.

service innovation, which ranked just slightly lower. These are clear findings—yet no country today has general standards that offer guidelines for measuring and reporting on the performance of these value drivers.

Nor do general standards exist for the last three value drivers, which the survey indicates to be in varying degrees less important to executives. The participating executives ranked *community involvement and environmental performance* lowest of all. The likely explanation is that U.S. companies in the aggregate—there are huge exceptions—have not had to confront a sustained environmental or community-focused protest or inquiry that chips away at a firm's pride and reputation. In instances where this has occurred, the impact on shareholder value and stakeholder approval has been very evident.

Here is the most critical point: Related research also showed that a very low percentage of the participating executives believed that their companies are providing a high level of public disclosure on any of the eight value driver categories.[3] Forty percent believed they were providing a high level of disclosure on product and service innovation and 34 percent said the same about product and service quality. Only 33 percent believed they were providing a high level of disclosure regarding "short-term financial information not required by GAAP." In brief, executives know what drives value and know that they do not communicate transparently to stakeholders on that basis.

DOES MANAGEMENT HAVE THE INFORMATION IT NEEDS?

Assume that management has articulated the true value drivers on which its strategy is based. It knows which ones are truly important, knows that it must manage them, and knows that it needs information about them to manage effectively. Therefore, the question is: "Does management have all the information it needs?" Ongoing research indicates that in many cases management does not have the right information.

The evidence again comes in surveys conducted by PricewaterhouseCoopers, specifically a set of surveys that offered executives in 10 industries lists of 25 to 35 value drivers compiled by experts in each industry.[4] Many of the listed value drivers were industry-specific, but for discussion purposes, most of these value drivers can be grouped in nine broad categories (see Exhibit 4.3 on p. 88). The executives were asked to rate the importance of each value driver and to rate the adequacy of their company's internal systems in providing information for reliable measures on each value driver. Whenever the difference between the two ratings proved to be large—i.e., when the measure is viewed as important but management has inadequate information on it—the survey identified that situation as a *Quality Gap*. Exhibit 4.3 shows these Quality Gaps by value driver and by industry.

The two empty columns and the cash flow column with only one check mark immediately draw the eye. Where earnings and segment information are concerned, the surveyed executives reported that they have adequate information. The same is true for information about cash flow, except for telecommunications. However, unlike the other industries where the question was about good information for the total company's cash flow, in the telecommunications survey the question was about whether reliable information existed for the more difficult measurement of cash flow by business segment. The strong coverage of earnings is in no way surprising

Exhibit 4.3
Quality Gaps By Industry

Industry	Market growth	Market share	Corporate strategy	Earnings	Cash flow	Segment information	Product innovation	Customers	Quality of management
Banking							•	•	•
Chemicals	•	•	•					•	•
Consumer products		•					•	•	•
High tech	•	•	•				•		•
Insurance	•						•	•	•
Investment management	•		•						•
Pharmaceuticals	•	•	•				•	•	•
Real estate	•		•				•	•	•
Retail	•	•							•
Telecommunications	•	•	•		•				•

Key: • Large Quality Gaps exist

Note: Industry specialists in the banking, insurance, and pharmaceutical industry have not identified cash flow as a key value driver. Therefore, this driver was not included in these surveys. Earnings were not included in the survey for Investment Management. In this industry, profit margin is used as a proxy for earnings.

because this information is required by GAAP, as is a cash flow statement. However, the finding that companies have excellent information about segments (e.g., business units) is quite striking. Analysts and investors typically clamor for more segment information beyond the required level of reporting. The survey—supporting common knowledge—indicates that companies collect and use this additional information, but many do not report it publicly.

In every industry surveyed, a Quality Gap appeared in the intangible but critically important category of *quality of management*. Since skilled management is indisputably a key value driver, stakeholders are justified in wanting information in this area. The hiring of a widely respected person as CEO or CFO—and, similarly, the dismissal of a senior executive who has failed to lead effectively—is capable of moving share price quite dramatically. Markets watch the top of the house and draw their own conclusions.

But management quality refers not just to visible leadership; it has to do with the entire organization, and companies that can demonstrate the high quality of their leaders and managers will gain in the marketplace. There is a role for reporting here. However, the survey indicates that companies in general do not collect adequate information on management quality for their own use, let alone for reporting purposes. The question of how to measure management quality is a difficult one, but one that every company should address, especially in the information it provides at Tier Three. One good way of doing so is by giving analysts and investors the opportunity to talk with and ask questions of senior executives. These conversations provide very useful input to analysts and investors, helping them to draw their own conclusions about the quality of the management team.

HOW WELL DOES MANAGEMENT KNOW HOW VALUE IS CREATED?

A deep understanding of how value is created is clearly important for executives. A PricewaterhouseCoopers Management Barometer Survey asked 156 executives about their interest in 15 business topics for future research. The top pick was business performance measures for building models that incorporate financial and nonfinancial information.[5] This is not a trivial finding.

Quite a few companies have already attempted to trace value creation from cause to effect—from value driver to measurable value result. In the survey on which Exhibit 4.2 is based, 69 percent of the executives surveyed reported that they had attempted to demonstrate empirical cause-and-effect relationships between the different categories of value drivers and both value creation and future financial results. Less than one-third of these felt they had truly completed the task;[6] this suggests its difficulty.

Still more challenging is to combine numerous cause-and-effect relationships into an overall business model that maps the holistic relationships across a set of different value drivers.[7] Here 61 percent had made at least a modest attempt, but only 10 percent felt they had really "nailed it."[8]

Establishing cause-and-effect relationships helps enormously when attempting to construct a business model. Of the executives who reported making some progress in demonstrating these empirical linkages, 78 percent of them also reported making progress in developing business models. In contrast, of the 31 percent who believed they had made little progress in establishing these relationships, only 24 percent also claimed to have made progress on the business-modeling task.[9]

The same survey compared companies that reported progress on identifying causal linkages and establishing holistic business models to companies that reported making little or no progress in this regard. The former group of companies reported a higher five-year historical growth rate in revenues, a higher growth rate in the period 2000 to 2001, and a higher anticipated growth rate for 2002.[10] Without question, companies that have grasped how to measure and manage their value drivers do a better job of delivering top-line revenue growth.

INFOSYS: A CONTEMPORARY BUSINESS MODEL, TRANSPARENT REPORTING[11]

There is no single, universally applicable format for business modeling. A company can express its business model as a detailed "value driver tree," a spreadsheet, graphics with an attendant set of measures, or in more intuitive terms.

Infosys (www.infy.com), a company based in Bangalore, India, defines itself as a consulting and information technology service provider, which offers its clients services in the areas of software development, maintenance, reengineering, package implementation, and other services such as consulting and software testing.

The company articulates its strategy on its website with a few graphic models and a detailed list of performance measures. The cornerstone of the company's strategy is described as a "delivery model" that leverages highly trained, lower cost domestic software development resources and maintains higher cost resources, as appropriate, closer to customers wherever they may be. Infosys reports that lower software development and maintenance costs represent a significant competitive advantage over other companies that pay much more for the same resources. This strategy is reflected in the company's graphically represented business model shown in Exhibit 4.4.

Infosys defines other important values driving its profitability. It reports that its focus on quality has made it possible for it to earn an external quality assessment of its software development process called SEI CMM level 5. According to the Software Engineering Institute (SEI), fewer than 80 organizations around the world currently have achieved this level.

Infosys believes that for stakeholders to understand whether its strategy can continue to deliver earnings

Exhibit 4.4
Infosys Business Model

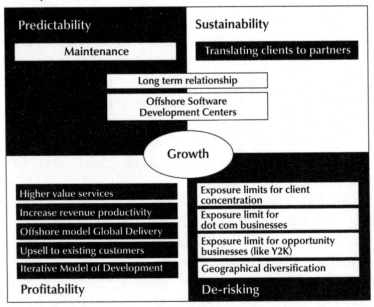

Source: Courtesy of Infosys, Bangalore, India.

growth and ensure the sustainability of its business model, stakeholders need information on other key performance measures. The following represent an illustrative list of such measures that Infosys provides to stakeholders to help them understand the profitability and sustainability of their business model:

- Profitability:
  - —Percentage utilization of resources.
  - —Average portion of support staff.
  - —Percentage of onsite versus offshore effort.
  - —Education index of all staff.
- Sustainability:
  - —Percentage of repeat business.
  - —Number of new clients added.
  - —Percentage of revenue from top 5 and 10 largest clients.
  - —Brand value.

The "Infosys intangible assets scoresheet" reports on the value of its human resources and of the Infosys brand.[12] The company reports this information externally, sharing the detailed calculations used to measure such things as brand value and human capital.

Infosys Founder and Chairman, N. R. Narayana Murthy, acknowledges the difficulty of developing the necessary performance measures, but he maintains that once this information is reliable enough to use for internal management purposes, it should be reported externally because "the company needs to live in harmony with all of its stakeholders."[13] He maintains that this high level of transparency in external reporting engenders trust in stakeholders of every kind. And he explains: "The softest pillow is a clear conscience."[14]

FROM MEASUREMENT TO RESULTS

Excellent strategies, well-identified value drivers properly measured, and a good business model are still not enough to create value for shareholders. Value is created when the right things get done. While information is a critically important guide to action, it must be used properly. That can happen when a company has an effective organizational design, rigorous enterprisewide risk management, sound compliance policies and procedures, and corporate governance that truly represents the interests of shareholders and other stakeholders.

A basic course on organizational design would not be welcome (or necessary) to readers of this book. Suffice it to say that three components required for an organization to function effectively in its pursuit of value creation are:

1. A sound organizational structure that specifies individual responsibilities and accountabilities.
2. Well-designed systems that produce the information people need to make decisions.
3. Incentives and rewards that recognize contributions made.

However, three other topics deserve brief discussion in the context of value drivers: enterprisewide risk management, compliance, and corporate governance.

ENTERPRISEWIDE RISK MANAGEMENT:
A VALUE DRIVER NEEDING
GREATER EMPHASIS

Although most companies manage risk to some degree, today only certain companies—typically those in financial services—consider it a key value driver. However, enterprisewide risk management (ERM) is slowly being recognized as an important value driver in a broader range of industries. Companies of many kinds are striving to understand more fully the relationship between decisions made and risks thereby entailed, which can either create or destroy value for shareholders.

The outcomes of decisions are uncertain, and this uncertainty creates risk, in terms of both upside opportunities and downside hazards. Failure to manage risk properly means that management exposes shareholders to unanticipated losses in value and may not identify ways to create more value. Management that fails to manage risk also relinquishes control of its company's destiny to outside forces. Shareholders understand that value creation requires risk-taking. They just want to know that potential value creation is proportionate to the level of risk and that potential downside losses are being managed intelligently.

Effective risk management at an activity, functional, or business unit level has three components. First, all risk elements must be identified, not only by assessing past experience, but also through creative thinking, brainstorming, and expert insight from inside and outside the company. Second, the identified risks must then be assessed. How likely are they? What are the consequences, both positive and negative? What forces can affect the likelihood or consequences of a risk factor? Third, decisions must be made about how to manage identified risks. Management can simply accept them. Or it can mitigate them by reducing their likelihood or consequences. Or it can transfer risk to others through insurance, hedges, and other means.

Effective enterprisewide risk management is based on taking an integrated approach to risk management across *all* of the company's activities, functions, and business units. This requires knowing the company's overall "risk profile" (the level of risk the company is willing to assume for the value it hopes to create), being able to assess its current risk profile, and making whatever adjustments are necessary. For certain types of risks, such as the exposure of an equity or bond portfolio, sophisticated "value-at-risk" measures exist. For others, such as operational risks in processing financial transactions, measurement methodologies are much less well developed. Thus, today's ERM is a combination of sophisticated quantitative techniques and effective management processes for strategic planning, budgeting, performance measurement, and internal control.

These management processes must be able to identify how capital has been allocated across the different parts of the company, the level and types of risk to which this capital is exposed, procedures for taking action when risk levels are too high, and whether risks in one part of the company exacerbate or ameliorate those in another. In order to do this, management must have a deep understanding of its company's value drivers, as discussed above, and of events that can affect the company in both positive and negative ways.

Management must then decide on acceptable tolerance levels and must be able to monitor them. For example, if customer satisfaction is an important value driver and customer satisfaction is affected by call center waiting time, a 15-second wait may be regarded as acceptable. But management needs to know when waiting time becomes 90 seconds in order to take appropriate action.

Fundamentally, ERM is about how management is using capital entrusted to it by the company's shareholders. Shareholders want to know if any decisions being made by management have a big enough downside to risk the company's solvency and push it into bankruptcy. In such circumstances, shareholders will expect the upside to be enormous. But management rarely "bets the company." More commonly, shareholders need simply to know whether management is taking intelligent risks with shareholders' capital in order to provide a return commensurate with the shareholders' risk as investors. Investors are willing to pay a premium for good management, and there is no good management without good enterprisewide risk management. In the end, creating value and managing risk are one and the same.

COMPLIANCE: A CORNERSTONE OF RISK MANAGEMENT

Another risk deserves special attention: the failure of individuals within a company, or of those with whom the company does business, to obey the rules—be those rules company policy, a code of professional conduct, government-mandated regulation, or the laws of the land. Managing this risk often falls under the somewhat chilling name of compliance, with its innuendo of forcing people to do things.

Compliance, properly managed, creates incentives (other than the threat of punishment) for doing the right thing. But even for people of the highest personal integrity, knowing exactly the right thing to do may not be simple due to complex laws and regulations that range, for example, across issues, industries, and countries or due to the complexity of contracts with customers and suppliers. Not knowing the right thing to do can also result from lack of clear communication to the right levels of the company about the company's strategy and value drivers.

The consequences to companies and their employees for compliance failure can be internal, such as strategies not executed properly. Or they can be external and sometimes harsh: financial penalties, tarnished reputations, legal liabilities, and even imprisonment. The public's appetite to see punishment meted out to those who have earned it will only escalate as investors and stakeholders become more sensitive to a company's transparency in its financial dealings and behaviors, both individual and collective.

CORPORATE GOVERNANCE: THE FOUNDATION OF GOOD MANAGEMENT

Keen attention is being paid today to corporate governance because that is where a culture of accountability begins and where it can be effectively fostered. What once seemed little more than a rubber stamp for executive decisions is now recognized as a value driver that can make or break a company. Recent experience has shown that boards, key members of the Corporate Reporting Supply Chain (Exhibit 4.5), need to pay attention; published accounts of some business failures have suggested that the board did not always conduct itself in exemplary fashion. A board's verbal commitment to safeguarding shareholder interests is one thing; living up that commitment is another.

Exhibit 4.5
Boards of Directors in the
Corporate Reporting Supply Chain

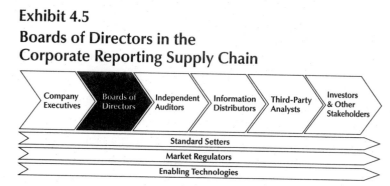

For the most part, boards of directors of public companies take seriously their corporate governance oversight responsibilities. Earnest or not, board members may fall short of their aims if they fail to devote the required time and do not have resources at their disposal to fulfill their role adequately. Fulfilling their role also requires not only a deep knowledge of the business, the industry, and the company's competitors, but also the individual courage to challenge management on critical issues when a board member disagrees with a decision or proposed direction.

Consider what board members should do:

- Satisfy themselves that the company's strategy will deliver value to shareholders.

- Determine whether the right value drivers have been identified, and that the business model makes clear their interactions.

- Evaluate the measures that monitor progress on value drivers and the quality of the information, both internal and external, used in producing those measures.

- Ensure that the board itself, particularly the non-executive directors, receives the information it needs, and that the information is reported to the company's stakeholders.

- Understand and assess the adequacy of the chosen organizational design for implementing the company's strategy and enterprisewide risk management program, and similarly understand and assess the effectiveness of the company's compliance program from the shop floor to top management and the board itself.

- Approve the company's financial statements prepared by management on which an independent audit opinion is given.

- Set compensation policies and amounts for senior executives.

Sometimes, unfortunately, nonexecutive directors who sit on boards—even of some of the world's most prestigious companies—do not devote the time necessary to fulfill properly their obligations to shareholders. Nor do they always have the necessary staff support to do so, especially when compared to the resources readily available to executive board members.

If nonexecutive directors allow themselves to serve as rubber stamps for the corporate executives who appoint them (with only perfunctory ratification by shareholders), executives so inclined can manage the board in the same way they manage market expectations about earnings. If directors receive only a portion of the full range of the information they need, or too much information too late, or information in an unusable format, they cannot possibly have enough knowledge to fulfill their role.

Unfortunately, experience has shown that some executives do not sincerely believe in or want good corporate governance. They view it as a constraint on their ability to make their preferred decisions. Sometimes they genuinely regard these decisions as in the best interests of shareholders, but at other times they know full well that their decisions are designed strictly to further a short-term goal such as driving up the stock price. They hope that the negative long-term consequences almost certain to follow will occur after they are long gone.

A commitment to good corporate governance is the true test of management's commitment to transparency, accountability, and integrity. If management is not honestly transparent with its own board, how can it practice external transparency with shareholders and other stakeholders? If management is not willing to be held accountable by the board, how can it have the legitimacy to hold accountable others in the company? Finally, if management does not exemplify integrity, how can it possibly attract people of integrity to its ranks?

A company without integrity destroys shareholder value and undermines public trust in the entire Corporate Reporting Supply Chain. Enron offers the tragic example of a company that lost public trust by allowing its integrity to be called into question. The future of corporate reporting and of public trust depends on keeping such disasters to an absolute minimum.

Yes, companies will continue to fail. This is a natural part of the "creative destruction" on which markets depend. Shareholders will continue to lose money when companies fail. But these failures and losses should happen only because management and strategies go awry. Failures and

losses must not happen because corporate reporting con-
cealed the truth.

NOTES

1. PricewaterhouseCoopers, "PricewaterhouseCoopers Management Barometer Survey: Nonfinancial Measures are
Highest-Rated Determinants of Total Shareholder Value" (hereafter referred to as Management Barometer Survey), news
release (New York: PricewaterhouseCoopers), April 22, 2002.
Also see www.barometersurveys.com/pr/newsflash_mg.html.

2. The authors would like to thank Professors Christopher
Ittner and David Larcker of the Wharton School at the University
of Pennsylvania for their help in designing this survey.

3. Management Barometer Survey.

4. See ValueReporting Web site, www.valuereporting.com.

5. Based on PricewaterhouseCoopers Management Barometer Survey conducted in the first quarter of 2001. Unpublished.

6. Management Barometer Survey.

7. For some hypothetical examples of business models, see
Eccles, *The ValueReporting Revolution,* Chapter 1.

8. Management Barometer Survey.

9. Ibid.

10. Ibid.

11. Descriptions of certain companies' reporting and ex-
tracts from third-party publications have been included in this
book as selective examples of reporting along the lines discussed. This third-party information, therefore, has been taken
out of context from its original publication, and readers are cau-
tioned to bear this in mind. Inclusion of certain companies as
examples does not imply any endorsement of such companies or

any verification of the accuracy of the information contained in the examples. Furthermore, the forward-looking statements mentioned in some of the examples were qualified by a "hold harmless" statement in their original publication.

12. Infosys Annual Report 2001, www.infy.com/investor /reports.asp. The annual report states that "The score sheet published by Infosys is broadly adopted from *The Intangible asset score sheet* provided in the book titled *The New Organizational Wealth* written by Dr. Karl-Erik Sveiby and published by Berrett-Koehler Publishers, Inc., San Francisco."

13. Eccles interview: N. R. Narayan Murthy, founder and chairman of Infosys, April 3, 2002.

14. Ibid.

CHAPTER FIVE

CORPORATE REPORTING

The corporate reporting of few, if any, companies today provides the disclosure contemplated by the Three-Tier Model of Corporate Transparency and, within that model, the information requirements of Tiers Two and Three. This is not surprising. Corporate commitment to greater transparency is still in its infancy, although it is maturing rapidly. Committing to transparency requires believing that its benefits will outweigh its risks and costs. Companies cannot wait to start practicing greater transparency until it has been thoroughly field-tested in a simulated capital market. They have to start practicing it now, in the real world, in real time.

Turning a general commitment to transparency into a specific managed process is more difficult still. Very few companies have volunteered to go transparent first, although some have taken the initial steps, and some even acknowledge that real competitive advantage can accrue to companies that go down this path. Those willing to start the journey are growing in number, as examples later in this chapter show. Those still hesitant at the starting gate may find great benefit in heeding the example that others are setting.

Transparency in corporate reporting is easily enough described. Putting it into practice is the hard part. All stakeholders want high-quality information, delivered in a timely manner, and in a form they can use. They also want information that paints a complete picture of performance, updated as frequently as necessary.

To practice greater transparency and satisfy stakeholders, management must confront five major challenges:

- Model external reporting on internal reporting.
- Determine the information that stakeholders need.
- Report relevant information from external sources.
- Report on the real economic entity.
- Weigh the risks and costs against the benefits.

Company executives *must* meet these challenges, for they are responsible for the first link in the Corporate Reporting Supply Chain (Exhibit 5.1).

Exhibit 5.1
Company Executives in the Corporate Reporting Supply Chain

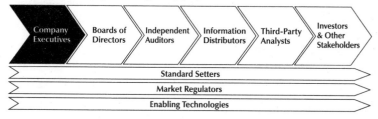

CHALLENGE #1: MODEL
EXTERNAL REPORTING ON
INTERNAL REPORTING

This first challenge is primarily an act of will. Management resolves that it will report externally much the same breadth of information that it uses internally to manage the company, concerning both historical performance and future goals and expectations. Not all internal information is relevant or appropriate for external stakeholders. Companies are better off, however, to start from the premise that they will provide all types of information and then ask themselves, "What will we not report, and why not?" The answers should be good ones and, in the spirit of transparency, they should be explicitly revealed. Shareholders will understand and applaud the decisions of fiercely competitive companies to refrain, for example, from publishing competitively sensitive information.

The logic of this reporting strategy is simple: The information that management finds useful for internal decision making is very likely also useful to those making decisions about whether to invest in the company, join it as an employee, supply it, buy from it, or allow it to operate in their communities. When companies base external reporting on internal management information, shareholders and other stakeholders know *what* management considers important in creating value and *who*—which business units or the corporate group, for example—is responsible for doing so.

Many companies must do two things to overcome this first challenge of transparency. They must stop playing The Earnings Game and they must ensure that they report the relevant information they use internally. Companies that play The Earnings Game try to create value by managing both the earnings expectations of the marketplace and actual reported earnings. When they do this, the disparity between the information they report externally and the information they use internally is often large. Radical though it may seem to many, information reported externally can truly reflect information used internally.

THE EXAMPLE OF USA NETWORKS

USA Networks, Inc. (www.usanetworks.com), an interactive commerce company, has announced that it is eliminating any disparity between internal and external numbers.[1] The company issued an extraordinary press release on October 24, 2001, stating that it no longer planned to engage in the "guidance ritual." Instead, the company said, "USA will provide the investment community with our actual internal budget, broken down by business segments."[2]

In commenting on why his company made this decision, Barry Diller, Chairman and CEO, said, "We have a rigorous process for budgeting for the future. We will simply publish the information, and update it quarterly. That's how we manage our business. And we'd rather be doing that than managing the Street."[3]

The company also announced its intention to communicate the assumptions used in preparing its budgets. While the company's general practice is not to revise these budgets during the year, in rare circumstances when it does so, it says that it will inform the market.

If USA does not provide guidance on earnings but, instead, posts its budgets and actual results, effectively it will make the internal the external. This is a level of transparency that cannot exist when a company's internal reporting is cloaked behind an external reporting system that has little to do with how the company is actually managed.

Once a company withdraws from The Earnings Game, the second thing management must do is to provide the relevant information it uses internally. It need not report with the same degree of internal detail, and some information will naturally be withheld as insignificant or competitively sensitive. But if there is a broad category of information that management considers important in managing the company, that information should be reported publicly. Few companies as yet follow this practice.

GAPS IN REPORTING

Consider once more the 10 industry surveys conducted by PricewaterhouseCoopers. Each of these surveys identified significant gaps between what management said it finds important in running the company and what, by its own admission, it actually reports to the public. These are *Reporting Gaps*. Exhibit 5.2 lists the industries in which the survey series revealed large Reporting Gaps for nine broad categories of value drivers.

In every industry surveyed, Reporting Gaps were found in information about customers and quality of management. This can largely be explained by the Quality Gaps discussed in Chapter 4, which occur when management either does not have the information, as would be the case for quality of management (no one yet knows how to properly quantify this measure), or considers its information not reliable enough to report publicly.

Not surprisingly, as evidenced by few or no Reporting Gaps, management perceives that it actively provides information on earnings, cash flow (telecommunications is the

Exhibit 5.2
Reporting Gaps By Industry

Industry	Market growth	Market share	Corporate strategy	Earnings	Cash flow	Segment information	Product innovation	Customers	Quality of management
Banking	•		•					•	•
Chemicals			•				•	•	•
Consumer products		•	•				•	•	•
High tech	•	•					•	•	•
Insurance	•		•				•	•	•
Investment management	•		•			•	•	•	•
Pharmaceuticals							•	•	•
Real estate							•	•	•
Retail	•	•				•	•	•	•
Telecommunications	•		•		•	•		•	•

Key: • Large Reporting Gaps exist

exception here), market share, and segment information (with three exceptions each). In the case of telecommunications, the survey question was about reporting cash flow by business segment, a more difficult task that represents a higher level of transparency.

Quality Gaps may partially explain Reporting Gaps in these performance measures. But Reporting Gaps also occur because management simply does not report information even though it could. When this occurs, stakeholders are deprived of complete information and must make decisions on the basis of a narrower range of company-reported information, perhaps supplemented with information from other sources. The accuracy and reliability of this other information is, of course, beyond management's control.

CHALLENGE #2: DETERMINE THE INFORMATION THAT STAKEHOLDERS NEED

The second major challenge of transparency is to ensure that management indeed communicates the information that stakeholders need, in a format as useful as possible. At the very least, management should report this information in paper documents and post it on a Web site in an organized and logical way. As Chapter 6 emphasizes, the most commonly used formats today are light years away from making information truly usable. Those who relegate important information to footnotes in an annual report, post it in an obscure Web site location, or bury it deep in a 100-page document do not adhere to the spirit of transparency even if the content—the substance of the information—is reported.

Gaps in information

Reporting the information that stakeholders need requires knowing what this information is in the first place. The 10 PricewaterhouseCoopers industry surveys offer evidence that the market is dissatisfied with the information it receives, though it is interested in the same value drivers as management, albeit with some differences in emphasis. Exhibit 5.3 on page 112 shows where *Information Gaps* exist. Information Gaps occur when external stakeholders—in this case, institutional investors—regard certain information as important but do not believe that the company reports the information well enough. As was true for Reporting Gaps (information not reported by a company although management thinks this information to be important), significant Information Gaps occur across all of the industries surveyed, and they tend to occur most frequently for nonfinancial value drivers.

Exhibit 5.3 shows an overwhelming, though not surprising, number of Information Gaps across industries. The only information that investors across the board find satisfactory is earnings, and even in this regard the high-tech industry is perceived to fall short.[4]

Information Gaps occur in every industry surveyed concerning customers and the quality of management, a finding consistent with Reporting Gaps in each of the 10 industries. Investors are dissatisfied because companies are not making available to them information they consider to be important.

In other areas, companies think more highly than investors do of their reporting. Consider segment information: In every industry except telecommunications, investment management, and retail, management perceives itself to be

Exhibit 5.3
Information Gaps By Industry

Industry	Market growth	Market share	Corporate strategy	Earnings	Cash flow	Segment information	Product innovation	Customers	Quality of management
Banking	•					•		•	•
Chemicals			•			•	•	•	•
Consumer products	•		•		•	•	•	•	•
High tech	•	•	•	•	•	•	•	•	•
Insurance	•					•		•	•
Investment management	•	•	•		•		•	•	•
Pharmaceuticals	•		•			•	•	•	•
Real estate	•				•		•	•	•
Retail	•					•	•	•	•
Telecommunications	•	•	•		•	•	•	•	•

Key: • Large Information Gaps exist

doing a good job of reporting segment information. Yet in two of the industries mentioned and in six others—where management says it does a good job—investors say that they do not receive the information they want. Why? Perhaps because of the quality of the information reported, its timeliness, or its usefulness.

KNOWING THE GAPS

The only way a company can know if it adequately meets the information needs of stakeholders is to ask them through surveys, for example, or direct dialogue. Royal Dutch/Shell Group of Companies seeks input from its stakeholders about how well the company is meeting its commitment to sustainability. The company does this both through face-to-face communications and through a Web site (www.shell.com) where comments and criticisms are recorded and answered. If this is accomplished, the company will *know* that it knows what stakeholders want, rather than imagining that it knows.[5]

CHALLENGE #3: REPORT RELEVANT INFORMATION FROM EXTERNAL SOURCES

The information that stakeholders might want goes well beyond what a company can generate from its internal financial information systems. Frequently, a company must go outside its own boundaries to gather information for internal analysis and decision making and, in turn, to report externally. Only with this information can the company paint a complete picture of just how well it is performing against industry trends, for example, or against specific competitors (benchmarking).

A classic example of important externally gathered information is information on market growth, historical and projected. Enthusiastically reporting 10 percent growth last year misleads if the industry as a whole grew by 20 percent. The same holds true for reporting 12 percent growth as an ambitious goal if the market expects to grow by 19 percent.

The sources of information needed for measuring and projecting market growth vary by industry but typically include government agencies, trade associations, and research firms. The challenge for companies lies in gaining access to this information, assessing its quality, incorporating it into internal information systems (this is especially challenging if the information must be manually transcribed), analyzing it, and then making the results available to stakeholders in a timely and useful way. These are daunting tasks, but they are made possible, and in part easy, through the new technologies discussed in Chapter 6.

It is not surprising, therefore, to see that in nine of the industries surveyed large Information Gaps exist on market growth. In eight industries, executives admit that there are Quality Gaps relating to the availability and reliability of the information available internally. That a Quality Gap exists without a Reporting Gap in an industry like chemicals suggests that sometimes companies report information even though they are not sure it is all that reliable. Conversely, some companies in the banking industry do not report on market growth even though they possess what they regard as reliable information about it.

CUSTOMERS

Another telling example of the importance of external information relates to the broad value driver of customers. Information on customer retention and customer penetration can sometimes be generated, albeit with great difficulty, from a company's internal information systems. Customer satisfaction and customer "share of wallet," on the other hand, require data from external sources—from customers themselves, for example. Most industries are in the very early stages of establishing reliable methods for measures about customers. The fact that Information Gaps, Reporting Gaps, and Quality Gaps exist on the value driver of customers across industries surely attests to the difficulties of gathering reliable customer data and converting it into meaningful information for external reporting.

THE EXAMPLE OF TELSTRA

Difficult as the task may be, some companies make the attempt. Telstra Corporation Limited (www.telstra.com.au), an Australian telecommunications company, has taken extraordinary steps to identify, monitor, and report on customer satisfaction. In November 2000, the company set out its commitment to define levels of service in what it calls its Customer Service Charter, drafted with input from Telstra's Consumer Consultative Council. From the outset, Telstra also announced its commitment to regularly monitor and review its performance against the Charter and to publish an annual performance review. In addition, Telstra engaged PricewaterhouseCoopers to review and report on the development of both the Charter and Performance Review 2001.[6]

CHALLENGE #4: REPORT ON THE REAL ECONOMIC ENTITY

Recent and well-publicized corporate failures, most notably the Enron bankruptcy, have focused public attention on the extent to which self-serving definitions of the boundaries of the entity subject to reporting requirements can lead to disaster. In a networked economy, replete with alliance partners and outsourcing arrangements, scribing a hard line around a company in such as way as to clearly define where corporate responsibilities begin and end becomes increasingly difficult. Complete information—at Tiers One, Two, and Three—on the real economic entity diminishes the importance of precisely defining the entity for accounting purposes by providing investors and stakeholders with the ability to assess a company's economic, environmental, and social performance, and its future prospects, beyond the boundaries of ownership. If the relevant information is provided on each of these related entities, stakeholders can "consolidate" this information along with that from the company in whatever way they find most meaningful for their analysis.

Generally accepted accounting principles (Tier-One information) currently furnish an incomplete guide concerning how to define and report on the real economic entity, particularly if the scope of that entity extends beyond traditional financial reporting. In today's world, questions abound as to what should be consolidated into a company's reporting, how to define "material" relationships, how to identify and quantify risk and return, and other complex issues. Executives need to think carefully about what type of information should be reported on the real economic entity at all three tiers.

Drawing the boundaries around the real economic entity, where direct relationships have many forms and indirect relationships can be equally important, is a matter of judgment. No definitive rules can or should be established, because such rules would be likely to define hard-and-fast

IN SEARCH OF THE REAL ECONOMIC ENTITY

The issue of the real economic entity has gained visibility as a key and urgent consideration. While the board of directors must evaluate and decide on the perimeter of the real economic entity, here are some common examples of how some companies may expand those perimeters:

- *Subcontracting to lower manufacturing costs.* Apparel and shoe companies often subcontract to manufacturing plants in developing countries where working conditions and environmental compliance may not satisfy general international expectations. Reporting forthrightly on efforts to monitor and, where necessary, improve the subcontractors' adherence to expected policies has proven critically important to a company's reputation and brand.

- *Subcontracting to lower fixed costs and focus on product development and marketing.* High-tech firms, especially, have made this a fairly common practice. Performance information on these subcontractors is as relevant as it would be if the firms performed these functions in-house.

- *Selling through distributors.* The beverage industry does this routinely, as do many companies in the electronics industry. Astute investors want to know the inventory levels, accounts receivable, and accounts payable of distributors to assess if the reporting company's revenue projections are reasonable or not.

- *Outsourcing of information technology (IT).* More and more companies are outsourcing their IT function to application service providers (ASPs). In the heyday of the dot-coms, many ASPs did a substantial portion

(Continued)

of their business with new companies. When such a company could not meet its financial obligations and filed for bankruptcy, so did some of the ASPs—to the dismay of their other customers. Knowing more about other companies with which an alliance partner conducts business can be relevant to the reporting company's own performance.

- *Outsourcing research and development.* This type of outsourcing occurs, for example, among large pharmaceutical companies that fund smaller biotechnology firms to conduct initial, high-risk research. Information about the smaller firm—its capitalization, intellectual property rights, and marketing rights, for example—is relevant to the pharmaceutical company's return on capital.

boundaries, which ironically would invite some companies to "play games." A better solution is to let this responsibility rest with the company's board of directors. The board should ensure that it knows about all relevant relationships comprising the real economic entity, that it understands the shape and dynamics of the value chain of the business and related risk exposures, that it is getting the necessary information on them, and that this information, where appropriate, is being made available externally.

CHALLENGE #5: WEIGH THE RISKS AND COSTS AGAINST THE BENEFITS

While management has historically exaggerated the additional costs of greater transparency, which continue to decrease, and underestimated its benefits, which continue to increase, companies may have legitimate reasons not to disclose certain information (unless required by regulation). Certain disclosures might put the company at a competitive disadvantage. They might be easily misleading. Some information might be unreliable, too detailed to be clarifying, or ultimately, and in all sincerity, too costly to assemble. Unfortunately, managers have no simple equations for calculating the trade-offs between the costs of greater transparency and its benefits. As with defining the boundaries of the real economic entity, sound judgment is required here, too.

Again, the role of the board of directors is central. As the representatives of shareholders, directors are responsible for identifying all relevant information that external stakeholders legitimately need or want. If management argues against making certain information available, the board has the right and responsibility to agree or disagree. This implies that in making such a decision the board fully understands the industry in which the company operates, its competitive position, the impact of potential litigation, the company's performance track record, and the market's current perception of management credibility.

In making judgments about whether or not to disclose information, two overriding principles apply. The first is openness. If the decision is not to disclose certain information, management should clearly and publicly communicate why it has made this decision.

The second principle is consistency. Once the decision has been made to report certain information, the information should be reported in good times and bad. If information is not to be disclosed, management should not reconsider its decision when short-term advantage might be gained by reporting it. Management might legitimately and publicly take the view that market share information is too sensitive to report because of competitive risk. But to turn around and announce a 10 percent increase in market share, with the hope of raising share price, would be disingenuous. Management can always reconsider its policy and choose to start—but must continue—to make this information available. Inconsistency can raise questions about the quality of all information reported. Investors will believe, often rightly so, that the company is more interested in impression management than performance management.

There are few, if any, better examples of candid reporting than that of Berkshire Hathaway, Inc. (www.berkshirehathaway.com). The company's CEO, Warren Buffett, has become legendary for his frank style of reporting. For example, one of the company's business principles states: "We will be candid in our reporting to you, emphasizing the pluses and minuses important in appraising our business value. Our guideline is to tell you the business facts that we would want to know if our positions were reversed."[7]

Mr. Buffett delivers on that promise in his 2001 Chairman's letter: "Though our corporate performance last year was satisfactory, *my* performance was anything but. I manage most of Berkshire's equity portfolio, and my results were poor, just as they have been for several years. Of even more importance, I allowed General Re to take on business without a safeguard I knew was important, and on September 11th, this error caught up with us. I'll tell you more about my mistake later and what we are going to do to correct it."[8]

THE FULL ARRAY OF INFORMATION: THE VALUEREPORTING FRAMEWORK

To confront the five challenges of achieving greater transparency, a further challenge awaits management: reporting to shareholders and stakeholders in a logical and organized way all the information it has decided to disclose. Stakeholders are not data miners. They require and deserve clear, logically presented information. The ValueReporting Framework (Exhibit 5.4) offers a solution that companies can use for organizing the information they report to stakeholders. Developed on the basis of PricewaterhouseCoopers' capital market research, it provides a comprehensive means of structuring internal and external reporting.

This framework presents four basic categories of information. Together they create a coherent and complete medium-term picture of a business, against which short-term

Exhibit 5.4
The ValueReporting™ Framework

External	Internal		

Market Overview	Value Strategy	Managing for Value	Value Platform
• Competitive environment	• Goals and objectives	• Economic performance	• Innovation
• Regulatory environment	• Organizational design	• Financial position	• Brands
• Macro-economic environment	• Governance	• Risk management	• Customers
		• Segmental performance	• Supply chain
			• People
			• Corporate reputation

financial performance can be explained. The framework builds on a number of underlying principles, foremost among them the notion of transparency. It assumes that shareholder interests are primary, but recognizes that long-term sustainable value is realized only if the interests of all stakeholders are understood and addressed.

The four categories of the framework link to and build on one another. For this reason, the framework should not be viewed as a static medium for presenting discrete bits of information. Used properly and integrated into internal management processes, it becomes a dynamic tool for assessing and monitoring all key aspects of performance and for communicating publicly their contribution to value creation.

Few, if any, companies have fully adopted all of the ValueReporting concepts. However, a small but growing number of companies have begun to embrace its principles, and some instructive examples within specific categories of the framework can be found worldwide. One example for each of the four framework categories is briefly described in the next few paragraphs. Many more examples appear in the *ValueReporting Forecast,*[9] published annually by PricewaterhouseCoopers. Transparent reporting about a particular piece of information is not the same as a high overall level of transparency. Nor is it the same as creating value for shareholders, which is ultimately based on performance, not on transparency per se.

MARKET OVERVIEW

In this category, management reports its assessment of the competitive and regulatory environment, including the broader macro-economic environment in the geographies where it does business. This type of information relates primarily to Tiers Two and Three of the model presented in Chapter 2, in that much of it varies by industry and often by individual company.

While most of this information comes from sources outside the company, management must shoulder responsibility for assessing its accuracy and specifying sources. When the information comes from within the company and represents management's assumptions and calculations, this too should be made clear. Naturally recognizing that assumptions and judgment are involved, stakeholders want to know management's view so that they can then form their own opinions about the external environment and decide whether management has been too optimistic or pessimistic about it.

Example: Noranda (www.noranda.ca), Canada[10]

For each of the four most important metals it mines, this mining company describes the dynamics of its marketplace—for example, global production versus consumption—and the drivers of each, including inventory levels and metal prices. Predictive commentary is given about the market outlook. The company also provides a sensitivity analysis through a chart that shows the annualized impact on the company's net earnings of a 10 percent change in metal prices. The company reported that a 10 percent change in the 2001 fourth-quarter average zinc price would affect Noranda's annual after-tax earnings by approximately $43 million.

VALUE STRATEGY

In this category, management explains to stakeholders how the company intends to create value. A description of strategy communicates the company's quantitative and qualitative goals, the organizational structure in place for implementing the strategy, and the governance function that oversees management's activities against that strategy. Most of the information here is Tier Three in nature, although this too may vary by geography.

The strategy should take account of the needs and concerns of all stakeholders whose views and actions can affect the long-term sustainability of the company. In its communications, management should explicitly describe how it understands and foresees the impact of various types of stakeholders on shareholder value.

Example: Royal Dutch/Shell Group of Companies (www.shell.com), the Netherlands/United Kingdom[11]

Shell, in its *People, planet and profits: The Shell Report 2001,* extensively describes how it uses its sustainable development framework in its efforts to create value for the future, and narrates actions taken to meet its economic, environmental, and social responsibilities. This framework of policies, standards, and guidelines not only covers areas such as financial control and accounting, information management, and use of the brand, but also covers issues such as human rights, climate change, and biodiversity. Shell identifies the following benefits of a strategy informed by sustainable development: attracting and motivating top talent, reducing cost through eco-efficiency, reducing risk, influencing product and service innovation, attracting more loyal customers, enhancing the brand, and enhancing reputation. Shell considers its commitment to contribute to sustainable development a key part of its competitive edge.

MANAGING FOR VALUE

This category of the framework, linking strategy and the company's financial performance, focuses particularly on business segmentation, the relationship between risk and return, funding, and the ability to generate cash. Here the key elements of traditional financial statements should be analyzed and supplemented with other information such as return on capital, earnings after deducting the cost of capital, and risk-adjusted returns on capital.

A willingness to segment performance information is critical. The segmented information must reflect how the company is actually managed. Companies should also provide trend data, targets, and, where possible, relevant benchmark comparisons. Because the ultimate financial measure for shareholders is total shareholder return (TSR), companies should report on this, ideally in alignment with the internal metrics used to manage the business.

In relation to risk, companies should disclose the nature of the key risks facing each business segment, as well as how they manage those risks. Astute shareholders and other stakeholders understand that companies must take risks to create value. They simply need to know what the risks are, their upsides and downsides, and how the company manages them.

Example: The Boots Company (www.boots-plc.com), United Kingdom[12]

This retailer of "well-being products and services" identifies total shareholder return (TSR) as its "single unambiguous measure" of shareholder value and group performance. The TSR performance is monitored on a rolling five-year basis against 10 peer companies. The company explains why and how the composition of this peer group changes due to changes in the marketplace. The company is consistent in disclosing this peer group comparison, as demonstrated by the fact that the company's position decreased from number 6 on March 31, 2000, to number 7 on March 31, 2001.

VALUE PLATFORM

The information in this framework category covers the activities and relationships that underpin how the company creates value. These are often nonfinancial in nature—for example, product quality and customer loyalty. Increasingly, the company's key intangible assets (brands, R&D, product development processes, corporate reputation, and the quality of its management) come into play here. As Chapter 3 emphasized, the relative importance of each of these elements and how they are defined and measured varies by industry. Most of this information resides at Tiers Two and Three, for which standards rarely, if ever, exist today.

Example: Coloplast Group (www.coloplast.com), Denmark[13]

Coloplast, a medical disposables company, explicitly states that employee loyalty and motivation are vital to corporate growth. The company reports detailed information on the related value drivers (working conditions, employee development, and knowledge management) through a set of measures—for example, employee satisfaction, staff turnover and absence, and staff competence. Five-year historic information is shown. All of this is part of the annual report. The company reports its intention to implement a system for internal auditing of these data that can support an external auditing process in the future. Similar information is provided for customers, social responsibility, and environmental consciousness.

FROM CONTENT TO FORMAT

This description of the ValueReporting Framework has been communicated to the reader in a paper-based format—a book. Virtually everyone would agree that books, pamphlets, printed newspapers, and many other paper-based communication formats will not be superseded any time soon for the wide range of purposes they serve effectively. But corporate information, in all its growing quantity and complexity, *can be*—and in reality *must be*—communicated more effectively with the use of new technology. Reported information needs to break away from the constraints of paper-based formats. The next chapter describes how this can happen.

NOTES

1. On May 7, 2002, the company announced plans to change its name to USA Interactive.

2. USA Networks, Inc., "14% EBIDTA Growth From USA's Operating Businesses," press release (New York: USA Networks, Inc.), October 24, 2001.

3. Barry Diller, chairman and CEO, USA Networks, Inc., October 24, 2001, USA Networks, Inc. 3rd Quarter Media Conference Call. Also see www.usanetworks.com/investor.relations /conference.calls.html.

4. This may be due to the fact that at the time of this survey many of these companies did not have any earnings and the practice of reporting pro forma earnings was becoming widespread. In retrospect, many of these companies were never going to have any earnings because of flawed business models. At the time of this survey, which business models were good ones and which ones were not was not clear, but the existence of an Information Gap for strategy in the high-tech industry indicates some uncertainty and concern at the time which turned out to be well justified.

5. Eccles, *The ValueReporting Revolution*, 161–183.

6. Telstra Corporation, Ltd., "Customer Service Charter Performance Review 2001," *Telstra,* June 30, 2001. Also see www.telstra.com.au.

7. "Berkshire Hathaway, Inc., "Owners Manual," www. berkshirehathaway.com/2001ar/ownersmanual.html.

8. Berkshire Hathaway, Inc., "2001 Chairman's Letter," www.berkshirehathaway.com/letters/2001.html.

9. PricewaterhouseCoopers, *ValueReporting Forecast 2002: Bringing information out into the open* (London: Pricewaterhouse-Coopers, 2001). Also see www.valuereporting.com.

10. Noranda, Inc., *Annual Report 2001,* www.noranda.ca.

11. Royal Dutch/Shell Group of Companies, *People, planet and profits: The Shell Report 2001,* www2.shell.com/home/royal-en/downloads/shell_report_2001.pdf.

12. The Boots Company PLC, *Annual Report and Accounts 2001,* www.boots-plc.com/information/info.asp?Level1ID=5&Level2ID=9.

13. Coloplast Group, *Annual Report 2000/2001,* www.coloplast.com/ECompany/CorpMed/AnReport/Homepage.nsf/(VIEWDOCSBYID)/F231DE184AA35BA341256ADB00399AD9.

CHAPTER SIX

THE INTERNET

Every aircraft in the world would be grounded if air traffic control relied on the same type of system that companies use today to report their information. Air traffic controllers must receive vast amounts of highly technical, constantly changing information reported to them quickly in a format they can understand and use immediately, and they must have absolute trust that the information is complete and accurate every time. Imagine the consequences if those controllers could only get their information from an observer on the ground who scribbled a few notes, printed them on an old-fashioned press, and mailed the information to the control tower once a quarter? Like air traffic controllers, investors cannot make critical, timely decisions if information is withheld, delayed, buried inside other irrelevant information, or presented as complex raw data. Yet, this is what investors must contend with today. Because current reporting formats provide too little too late, those who use corporate information typically turn to second-hand sources, none of them comprehensive or totally objective, some of dubious reliability.

To offset this inventory of problems, here are some promising "what-ifs." What if companies used the Value-Reporting Framework described in Chapter 5 to organize their information? What if they communicated that information on a much more timely basis? What if they could report in a way, both internally and externally, that virtually eliminated the effort, cost, and risk of using information? If companies could do all that, they and all other participants in the Corporate Reporting Supply Chain would have passed a major milestone in creating the future of corporate reporting.

THE INTERNET: A TOOL IN NEED OF SHARPENING

Most companies and their stakeholders already use the Internet to publish and obtain performance information, to share it with others, and to analyze it. Investors, especially, expect the information that companies report on the Internet to be of high quality, quickly accessible, and easy to use. Most important, they expect it to be trustworthy. Yet those expectations are rarely, if ever, met in the current Internet environment.

This chapter explains why that is so and describes the resulting consequences and constraints imposed on companies and stakeholders. It also speaks to the enormous benefits that new Internet technologies, available now, can offer to the Corporate Reporting Supply Chain.

What remains is for the supply chain participants to embrace these solutions. They need to understand much more fully how incorporating advanced Internet technology at every possible step can enhance transparency and build greater public trust.

CONTENT AND FORMAT

What companies report (the content) and how they report it (the format and presentation) are integrally linked. When the format enables stakeholders to understand the content more easily, they use that content more effectively. The evolution of information formats—from clay tablets and printed paper to e-mail, Web sites, and pdf files—has progressively made content more accessible, understandable, and useful. The linkage of content to format has never been more crucial than now, when the Internet is quickly becoming the primary platform for communication and commerce.

In using the Internet today, however, the Corporate Reporting Supply Chain has essentially duplicated the paper format, with all of its limitations, in the new electronic environment. Corporate reporting on paper or its electronic equivalent, no matter how good the content, will not suffice in today's—let alone tomorrow's—environment.

LIMITATIONS OF PAPER-BASED FORMATS

No matter how sophisticated its graphics or how many hyperlinks to more information it may offer, most corporate information on the Internet still appears and functions much like a piece of paper pasted to a computer screen. Reusing what is read—for example, transferring data to a spreadsheet for analysis—almost always requires manually transferring the data to another format. This is a labor-intensive, time-consuming process, and the reuse of data is central to the activities of thoughtful investors and other stakeholders.

There are other problems. Electronically delivered information that mimics paper formats is inherently opaque, in the sense that users cannot see through or beyond the format. Users get little or no help in analyzing and understanding a document's content or in verifying its accuracy and authenticity. The term WYSIWYG—what you see is what you get—is not a virtue here. What you see is unfortunately *all* you get. And what you get may not be reliable, as will be demonstrated later.

Paper is not all bad. After thousands of years, it still works well for certain purposes. Corporate information on the Internet certainly offers advantages over paper—although not nearly as many as it could. The Internet speeds up the push (publishing information) and the pull (discovering and retrieving it). The problem is with the paper-like format. This can be vastly improved to save a great deal in terms of time, dollars, and intellect expended to acquire and use information.

LIMITATIONS OF COMPUTERS

Humans are adept at recognizing patterns in information, extrapolating meaning, and putting what they have learned into proper context. Computers are less able, on their own, to do these things unless the patterns in the information are consistent and recognizable or related to a set of existing rules. Computers, on the other hand, can process incredibly large volumes of raw data much more quickly and accurately than humans. While humans have relatively short attention spans and limited appetites for processing masses of raw data, computers do not get bored or tired.

Enabling the computer to understand both data and its context takes the computer's enormous processing power to the next level. Doing so requires giving the computer more explicit, descriptive information about the information it receives. This descriptive information (or, more correctly, descriptive data) is called "metadata"—data about the data. The melding of data and context is key to ensuring the trustworthiness of the information processed, and it is the foundation for a vast array of commercial uses, not the least of which is corporate reporting.

XBRL: A NEW LANGUAGE FOR CORPORATE REPORTING

Ironically, the shift to reporting corporate information over the Internet creates greater demand for even more information. As companies improve their ability to reach out to investors and other stakeholders, the market expects them to provide ever more timely and higher quality information.

As more information is generated, the stacks of electronic paper keep mounting. To break through this information overload and to use the Internet to its fullest advantage, the Corporate Reporting Supply Chain must adopt new technologies. It needs to eliminate the hand-tinkered, labor-intensive processes currently used for producing, reporting, and analyzing Internet-based information. What the supply chain needs is a new, universal language in which to report, and a way to use that language that does not require years of study.

The language exists. It is called XBRL[1]—Extensible Business Reporting Language. (See Exhibit 6.1.) Fortunately, the vast majority of Corporate Reporting Supply Chain members will never have to learn how to read or write XBRL. They will, however, need to know what XBRL does, which is to help solve the context and authentication problems of computers and to use the linkage of content and format to make the

Exhibit 6.1
XML: The Origins of XBRL

XBRL is a dialect of XML (Extensible Markup Language), a new Internet language that defines and names data. The World Wide Web Consortium (W3C)* recommended XML as a standard for Internet-based information in February 1998. It is potentially the most important Internet standard developed since the adoption of HTML, which gave birth to the Internet.

XML enables the exchange of data between disparate software applications through the use of informational tags that self-describe what a piece of information is. With XML, rather than search clumsily for words on a page, software applications can search for information that meets specific criteria, as described by the tags.

Because XML works independently of any software application, it can move information seamlessly between them. XML technology also offers:

- XML Digital Signature, which allows users to authenticate the source and integrity of the information presented
- Validation that information complies with pre-set rules
- Linkages to other relevant internal and external content

In sum, XML provides the foundation for the next phase of the global information revolution. It is being quickly adopted for commercial and private uses throughout the world.

*See: www.w3.org.

---

information that companies report more complete, higher quality, more useful, and more quickly received.

How does all this happen? XBRL delivers corporate information along with identification tags—the metadata described earlier—that make the information self-describing to a computer. In the past, if one computer sent another computer data on a company's $5 million in revenues, it transmitted the number 5,000,000 and the receiving computer would have to have already been programmed to recognize that number as revenue and to put it in a prede-fined revenue bin expressed in dollars, not cents or pounds. With XBRL, the figure 5,000,000 arrives with tags that say, "This number is revenues, as defined by Global GAAP number 18, measured in U.S. dollars for a specified period of time for this unique company." The receiving computer allows the information to flow automatically and seamlessly into its proper bin.

Investors and others can view and use that information as they choose—for example, to automatically compare a company's revenue to its profit, to prior-period revenues, or to another company's revenues. They no longer need to labor to transpose the sender's data manually into their own analytical software programs. As a result, the stake-holders' cost of consuming reported information decreases to a level approaching practically nothing.

BEYOND FINANCIAL INFORMATION

XBRL is not limited to the financial information at Tier One of the Three-Tier Model of Corporate Transparency. It can tag virtually any type of information, including the nonfinancial, industry-specific, and company-specific in-formation at Tiers Two and Three. It goes even further by facilitating the collection of information not only inside a company but outside as well. XBRL (and other XML di-alects) allows users to capture relevant information virtu-ally anywhere on the Internet and to reuse it easily—for example, in an internal management decision-making tool or an investor's analytical software.

The ability to gather contextually relevant information from outside of the company offers previously unattainable benefits to the Corporate Reporting Supply Chain. An often-cited problem with many reporting frameworks is management's inability to find and use high quality, performance-related information from sources external to the company. XML and XBRL solve the problem. Managers and investors who want market share or benchmarking information on customer satisfaction levels, for example, can glean it from an independent industry association's customer satisfaction survey data or from a customer complaints database maintained by a third party such as an oversight group in a regulated industry. XBRL can also enable or greatly facilitate reporting on the economic entities discussed in Chapter 5—for example, by collecting information on the inventory levels or accounts payable of a company's suppliers or distributors.

THE STATE OF XBRL AT MICROSOFT

XBRL is not vaporware. A fair number of prominent organizations and companies have already started publishing their information in the XBRL format, including Edgar-Online,[2] Microsoft,[3] Morgan Stanley,[4] and Reuters.[5] Microsoft's investor relations Website (www.microsoft.com /msft/) is widely regarded as today's state of the art. It offers investors enormous amounts of information and gives them the tools to use it. Recognizing that the state of the art must continuously advance, Microsoft has committed to a still more pervasive adoption of XBRL as its standard Internet reporting format and has set broad goals for its implementation, including:[6]

- To ensure the integrity and credibility of the company's financial information.

- To streamline and reduce the costs associated with preparing and distributing the company's financial information.

- To set an example and to promote XBRL's potential to benefit the entire marketplace.

- To benefit the company's stakeholder community.

The last goal is perhaps the most important. By adopting XBRL, Microsoft not only reduces its own costs, but also levels the playing field for the entire stakeholder community by offering everyone, from elite analysts to individual investors, the full picture of its financial condition.

Before XBRL, Microsoft duplicated its data dissemination efforts nearly every time it reported financial information—for example, in regulatory filings, on the company's Web site, or in printed financial statements. With XBRL, the company can virtually eliminate redundant data-gathering efforts previously required for every new purpose or audience. Microsoft gathers the data once and then reuses it again and again without ever having to regenerate it. "Publish once, reuse many times" is the new watchword.

An important point about ease of access and use: Investors and other stakeholders no longer have to visit Microsoft's Web site repeatedly to pull the company's data into their Excel worksheets. They can request the data from within their own worksheets, completely bypassing their browsers, and grab the information directly from the company's Web site. This gives them faster access and much more analytical flexibility than before.

THE CORPORATE REPORTING SUPPLY CHAIN, OLD AND NEW

To fully understand the benefits of adopting XBRL, it is helpful to look at the constraints and consequences of traditional reporting methods. Those constraints and consequences distribute themselves along the entire Corporate Reporting Supply Chain.

COST TO COMPANIES

As noted earlier, the cost to companies to report performance information, both internally and externally, is high. Internal systems for generating reports are often disparate and require manual interfaces and processes that impede the consolidation of information for decision making. The reports produced, whether paper or electronic, require human intervention at every turn, and the process generally results in information designed for a singular use.

In terms of production costs for business reports alone, XML-based Internet technologies can save companies as much as 60 percent over traditional publishing methods.[7] They can also greatly enhance the publishing process for those glossy printed annual reports that so many investors prize, and that corporate branding so often seems to require. Some companies are already achieving these cost savings by providing certain company reports exclusively over the Internet. Such is the case at American Life Insurance of New York (www.americanlifeny.com), which filed a required U.S. Securities and Exchange Commission (SEC) registration disclosure on its new variable annuity life policy offering exclusively on the Internet. This resulted in significant publishing cost savings (and it also required a special SEC authorizing order).[8] Others will surely follow this example.

STAKEHOLDERS PAY DEARLY FOR CONSUMING INFORMATION

The high cost of information consumption for stakeholders plays out in two ways: the cost of getting the information and the cost of turning it into something usable. Those who use corporate reporting information—investors, creditors, analysts, regulators, and a host of other stakeholders—spend much time reading a document just to find bits of information important to their purpose. Once they find it, they usually need to transpose it manually into an analytical software application. If they want to compare one company with others, they must go through the same time-consuming and error-prone process for each company.

On its corporate Web site, General Motors (www.gm .com) reports separate supplemental consolidated statements of income and other financial information on its Automotive, Communications Services, and Other Operations, and on its Financing and Insurance Operations. This is consistent with the concept of ValueReporting. But how long would it take just to find and read those separate statements, much less transcribe the data into a spreadsheet or analytic tool? Maybe up to half an hour for a skilled accountant or analyst? Who knows how long for the average individual investor?

The point is not to find fault with General Motors' reporting. The point is that the paper-like format, which the company has little choice but to use, makes working with the information laborious. Even when companies try to lessen the burden of reusing their information by providing it in electronic formats (like html for the browser, pdf for printing, or electronic spreadsheets), users are still disadvantaged. Each company has its own style of spreadsheet rows and columns. With no consistency in spreadsheet set up, users must reformat information to fit the requirements of their own analytical software. Given this obstacle course, investors often end up disregarding good available information and make decisions based on incomplete information.

XBRL will change all this. With faster access and greater reusability, investors can conduct more complete and timely analyses. They may still not make the right decisions—judgment matters here and everywhere—but they will have a formidable information set on which to base their decisions.

ANALYSTS ALSO BEAR THE CONSEQUENCES

Even sophisticated users like analysts can fail to incorporate all of the information available to them, some of it quite important. For example, companies are required to disclose the sensitivity of their defined benefit plan expense to market dynamics. That item of information is available to anyone who reads the notes to a company's financial statements. Yet during the bear market of late 2001, when the defined benefit plan expense of some companies increased, analysts and earnings watchers who failed to consider the disclosed information and its consequences were caught off guard.

This happens because many information distributors (whose role in the Corporate Reporting Supply Chain is to gather, consolidate, and disseminate company and other information, as shown in Exhibit 6.2) do not provide certain types of information. Transforming it from a paper-based report into an electronic format is simply too expensive. Analysts who get information from these distributors rely on them to provide information in a reusable format, and they simply may not have the time or resources to chase down information when it is not delivered in a reusable format.

Similarly, analysts are limited in how many companies they can cover because of the costs and time of getting and

Exhibit 6.2

Information Distributors in the Corporate Reporting Supply Chain

analyzing information on them. A paper, "The Road to Better Business Information: Making a case for XBRL," notes that, "Of the roughly 10,000 public companies in the United States, we estimate that only about one-third have any meaningful Wall Street research available. Because Wall Street research only covers the most actively traded stocks, huge gaps exist."[9] Logic argues that faster, easier access to reusable information will lead to increased analyst coverage of more public companies. This, in turn, could lead to more investors, greater liquidity, higher stock prices, and a better allocation of capital.

REDISTRIBUTED AND NORMALIZED INFORMATION

As just mentioned, once companies publicly report information, a vast network of third-party intermediaries (including, but not limited to, the information distributors) begins consuming and redistributing this information. Those who rely on information from third parties—typically investors and analysts—expose themselves to a wide range of potentially significant information risks, including distortion, time delays, and even fraud.

Almost all information reported by these intermediaries is done in a normalized manner. Normalization is a process of standardizing reported information into normal or standard categories for processing and distribution purposes. Information from different companies is treated identically. For example, different revenue recognition policies are not taken into account and a simple "revenues" figure is reported. The obvious reason for this is the cost of complexity introduced when every little nuance is considered. Such normalization often distorts or excludes some of the information the company originally reported. The process takes time and the information produced may have less value than the information the company originally reported.

On the other hand, normalization greatly increases the accessibility and often the reusability of information that survives the process. However, when investors believe that information has been distorted, they often strive to correct it. To this end, they contact the reporting company or other parties, and this detour increases their information consumption cost, just as it increases the information production cost of the company and other upstream participants in the Corporate Reporting Supply Chain. Again, XBRL helps here: The company tags information at the source, thus allowing its XBRL documents to speak for themselves, regardless of where the information is used.

More troubling is the potential for fraud in redistributed information. The very nature of how information is distributed, even through formal company channels, can sometimes expose companies and stakeholders to fraud. Emulex (www.emulex.com), a U.S. network storage company, and thousands of its stakeholders fell victim to this when a young man published a bogus press release through a news wire service to which he had access.[10] Reputable news distributors picked up the release and reported it to the market as authentic business information.

The company's stock value fell by an estimated $2.5 billion on the day of the bogus release.[11] The SEC estimated that overall investor losses exceeded $110 million.[12] To say the least, this incident raises the question of who is responsible for company information that enters the Corporate Reporting Supply Chain. Would it not be better for all concerned if investors could authenticate a press release at the time they receive it, regardless of the source?

INCOMPLETE, HIDDEN, AND DECEPTIVE INFORMATION

Management can maximize transparent reporting through XBRL. But XBRL cannot force management to report in a clear, complete, honest, and informative way; it is a format, not an enforcement agency. The graphics in reported information can misdirect and confuse the user, and some companies may deliberately hide information within volumes of details. Incompleteness can also result, as noted earlier, when third parties normalize information that may have been fairly complete when first reported.

Some potentially useful information that investors would value is not deliberately hidden—it is just inaccessible, or nearly so, without the tools discussed in this chapter. For example, as noted earlier in another connection, industry associations and regulatory bodies often publish market data that can be useful in benchmarking competing companies' performance. XML-based tools will open up tremendous storehouses of information, which today go largely unused, and the interoperability of this information—its convenient transfer from one application to another—will make it much easier for stakeholders to find their way to and through it.

DIFFERENCES IN SPEED OF ACCESS AND USE

Some stakeholders can receive and process reported information faster than others. This can result in incomplete information for some, at least during a critical time period, and may actually create opportunities for wrongdoing. The issue is information arbitrage. Speedier investors can make a good living out of being first to act in the market on the basis of new and often proprietary information. The more proprietary the information format—for example, delivered by a personal phone call from a company insider—the more difficulty others will have in using that information for their own decision making.

Regulators generally try to eliminate information arbitrage and reduce differences in information speed through initiatives such as the U.S. Securities and Exchange Commission's much discussed Regulation Fair Disclosure. Information speed depends in part on the reusability of reported information and, once again, XBRL can help.

REGULATION IS BURDENED, TOO

Many regulatory agencies around the world still use paper or paper-like electronic formats as the primary or preferred way to receive information from regulated entities. This results in manual regulatory processes that are prone to inaccuracies, habitually untimely, and quite costly to both regulators and those they regulate. The solution to this problem must now be obvious. Mercifully, in almost every major country e-government initiatives are under way to leverage the Internet, decrease the cost of regulation, and improve the overall regulatory process. This involves transforming the regulatory process to leverage Internet technologies, and in some specific instances XBRL.

The Australian Prudential Regulation Authority (APRA) (www.apra.gov.au) provides one good example of how XBRL allows information to be immediately transferred from one company to any other and be put to use at once. As each party in the Corporate Reporting Supply Chain agrees to publish and expect information in a standardized format, everyone can benefit.

APRA plans to begin providing companies with interactive regulation and direct feedback on their reported information compared to that of a peer group.[13] Regulated banks in Australia also provide information to APRA and will be able to immediately compare their information to the aggregated information of their peer group. This participatory regulation helps the banks to identify areas for improvement and makes the process more fully interactive.

Other regulators are evaluating similar processes. The Inland Revenue in the United Kingdom has decided to use the same information format as APRA for corporate income tax returns beginning in 2003,[14] as part of the foundation for its e-filing process. The Federal Deposit Insurance Corporation (FDIC) in the United States is pursuing a similar path for regulation of the financial services sector.[15]

SEE XBRL IN ACTION ONLINE

Readers who would like to see and actually interact with XBRL in a realistic environment can visit a demonstration site developed by Microsoft, Nasdaq, and Pricewaterhouse-Coopers (www.nasdaq.com/xbrl). The site draws on publicly available information from a number of companies in the semiconductor industry and provides tools that allow users to pull their financial data into a spreadsheet and to view and compare information across a wide variety of dimensions. This demonstration should persuade site visitors that XBRL is part of the future of corporate reporting. As it becomes more familiar, and as additional software tools become available to the mass market, investors will increasingly use it and insist on its use by companies in the Corporate Reporting Supply Chain.

THE QUESTION OF AUTHENTICATION

What possible downside could there be to making it easier to automatically create, publish, and obtain and reuse valuable information? Perhaps it is the concerns that go along with such ease. As investors, companies, and regulators increasingly use the Internet for business and market information, their trust in the integrity of the medium must be strengthened.

A trusting relationship exists when people know with whom they are dealing and can confidently assume that both parties adhere to a common code of values and behavior. On the Internet today, this foundation for trust remains somewhat shaky because nearly any site can be mimicked or willfully distorted without the knowledge of the company or investors. This was painfully evident in the Euroclear/Bloomberg $3.9 billion fraud,[16] when more than two-dozen

Internet sites and the documents they contained were fraud-ulently presented to investors. To a large degree, format defi-ciencies made this fraud possible because the electronic paper format provides virtually no solutions for investors to authenticate a document. XML-based tools will be available to help solve the problem. Technologies such as XML Digital Signature can automatically provide integrity, authentica-tion, and nonrepudiation of information presented in XBRL.[17]

Third-party assurance methodologies to meet the needs of the Internet-based Corporate Reporting Supply Chain must be designed. Although a complete toolkit does not exist, forward progress is evident. The use of XML Digital Signature to highlight what is covered by assurance, what is not covered by assurance, and how to provide and express that assurance are currently hot topics in R&D groups across the high-tech world.

MAKING THE PROMISE OF XBRL A REALITY

Realizing the benefits that XBRL promises (see Exhibit 6.3) requires a much closer integration of all the Corporate Re-porting Supply Chain participants. This type of integration is in many ways analogous to Henry Ford's innovation, the assembly line. It was the linchpin of Ford's success, giving birth to the Model T and driving the Industrial Revolution forward.

The assembly line was made possible by applying the most advanced production technology to Ford's manufac-turing systems. Suppliers could deliver parts, subassem-blies, and assemblies (themselves built on other assembly lines) precisely timed to a constantly moving main assem-bly line. This enabled Ford to turn out a complete chassis

Exhibit 6.3
XBRL: Cheaper, Better, Faster

For information preparers, XBRL helps to:

- Reduce the cost of preparing and publishing information (**cheaper**)
- Increase the speed and efficiency of business decisions, and provide real-time reporting to all stakeholders (**better**)
- Automate the migration of information from accounting systems to financial statements (**faster**)
- Improve internal reporting for management decisions (**better**)

For information consumers, XBRL will:

- Enhance access and reduce the cost of analyzing financial information (**cheaper**)
- Enables deeper analysis at any chosen level and reduce the margin for human error (**better**)
- Increase the speed of data use and related decisions (**faster**)

For all stakeholders, XBRL makes financial data:

- More accessible and easier to use (**better**)
- Easier to transfer (**faster**)
- More trustworthy when associated with an XML Digital Signature (**better**)

every 93 minutes, an enormous improvement over the 728 minutes formerly required.[18]

Similarly, integrating the Corporate Reporting Supply Chain will make it more efficient overall to the benefit of all the participants, particularly investors. Exhibit 6.4 graphically compares how XBRL enhances the consumption of corporate reports.

In Exhibit 6.4, the upper diagram depicts the Corporate Reporting Supply Chain today. Information from

Exhibit 6.4
How XBRL Changes the Consumption
of Corporate Reports

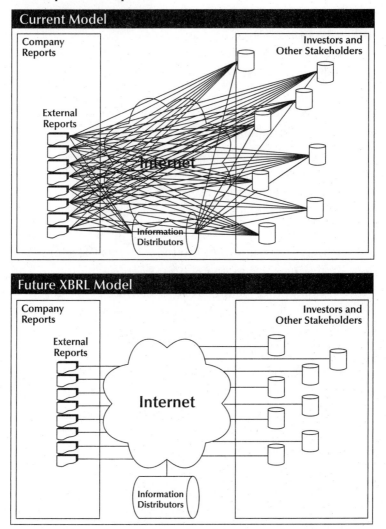

The consumption of corporate reports is transformed by the XBRL-enabled model. Investors will no longer have to retrieve opaque electronic paper documents from individual company Web sites and multiple information distributors, but will have access to information from any source on demand over the Internet. XBRL documents will allow many users, including the information distributor, to consume information in a very efficient manner over the Internet and conduct their analysis with timely, relevant, accurate, and complete information.

subsidiaries and business units goes through multiple con-
solidations until it reaches the report preparation process.
Generating the many internal paper-based reports needed
for management decision making requires labor-intensive
and costly processes.

Similar manual processes are required to generate the
multitude of external communications in paper-based formats—annual reports, quarterly reports, other regulatory
filings, news releases, Web site postings, investor briefings,
and more. External users—including those who consolidate
the external reports—must access each report individually,
read it, extract only the bits of information they want, and
re-enter the information into their spreadsheets and software programs for analysis. To compare information on several companies, the process must be repeated for each.

The lower diagram in Exhibit 6.4 depicts the simplification of the Corporate Reporting Supply Chain through
XBRL. Companies using XBRL can consolidate—efficiently and without manual processes—their subsidiary and
business unit information from many different sources and
systems. Consolidation happens automatically and information moves at the speed of light for internal management
decision-making purposes. At the same time, it moves externally through the Internet as investors, analysts, and other
stakeholders automatically request only the information
they need, which then flows into their spreadsheets and
software programs for analysis.

The XBRL information flow in the lower diagram ex-
emplifies "publish once and reuse many times." Investors
are no longer forced to retrieve opaque electronic paper
documents from individual companies. Timely, relevant, accurate, and complete information is available simultaneously to all for immediate use.

For XBRL to take hold in the global marketplace—across industry and geographic boundaries—the key participants must take the lead in developing it and adopting it as the standard in business reporting. But XBRL is only as good as the quality of the information on which it is based. This is why the assurance function plays such a critical role in building public trust.

NOTES

1. See www.xbrl.org/Faq.htm. PricewaterhouseCoopers is a leading member of the XBRL.org consortium, currently comprised of over 170 companies. PricewaterhouseCoopers was one of 13 founding member organizations, and its personnel have served in leadership roles such as Steering Committee Chairman, co-chairs, and chairs of a range of international working groups (Specification, Tools, General Ledger, Accountants, etc). PricewaterhouseCoopers proactively contributes leadership resources in moving this effort forward.

2. See www.edgar-online.com/investor/xbrl.asp.

3. Al Berkeley, John Connors, and Mike Willis, "The Road to Better Business Information: Making a Case for XBRL," white paper, Nasdaq, Microsoft, and PricewaterhouseCoopers. See www.microsoft.com/msft/XBRL/FinancialXBRLwp.htm.

4. See www.sec.gov/Archives/edgar/data/895421/ 000095013001500161 /ex99xbrlpilot.htm.

5. Reuters, "Reuters Takes the Lead in Reporting its 2001 Full Year End Financials," press release (Berlin, Germany: Reuters), March 4, 2002. Also see www.xbrl.org/News.htm.

6. Al Berkeley, John Connors, and Mike Willis, "The Road to Better Business Information."

7. Tad Leahy, "Reporting Online," *Business Finance,* October 2000, 55.

8. Harvey Pitt, Speech by SEC Chairman: Remarks at the PLI 33rd Annual Institute on Securities Regulation, New York, November 8, 2001. Also see www.sec.gov/news/speech/spch520.htm.

9. Al Berkeley, John Connors, and Mike Willis, "The Road to Better Business Information."

10. Brian Krebs, "Emulex Fraud Suspect Was Former Internet Wire Employee," *Newsbyte*, August 31, 2000. Also see www.infowar.com/law/00/law_083100b_j.shtml.

11. Terzah Ewing and Peter Waldman, "Emulex Is Victim of Internet Hoax," *The Asian Wall Street Journal*, August 28, 2000, 19.

12. CFO.com, "SEC Settles with Man who Created Bogus Emulex, Press Release," July 25, 2001. Also see www.cfo.com/article/1,5309,4319%7C%7CA%7C22%7C2,00.html.

13. "Statistics Project-Data Submission-XBRL," Australian Prudential Regulation Authority, April 30, 2002. Also see www.apra.gov.au/Statistics/XBRL.cfm.

14. PricewaterhouseCoopers and Walter Hamscher, "Inland Revenue CT E-Filing: The Business Case for XBRL," December 20, 2001. Also see xml.coverpages.org/Hamscher-IR-CT-efilingRev1.pdf.

15. XBRL.org, "XBRL International's new XML-based specification now being used by world's leading financial services institutions, government regulators and software developers," press release (Berlin, Germany: XBRL.org), March 5, 2002. Also see www.xbrl.org/News.htm.

16. International Chamber of Commerce, "CCS Foils Multibillion Dollar Internet Banking Fraud," *International Chamber of Commerce Commercial Crime Service News*, April 11, 2001. Also see www.iccwbo.org/ccs/news_archives/2001/fraud.asp.

17. For more information on how digital signatures work, see www.w3.org/Signature/Activity.html.

18. Fred Thompson, "Henry Ford," Atkinson Graduate School of Management, Willamette University, August 26, 1998. Also see www.willamette.edu/~fthompso/MgmtCon/Henry_Ford.html.

CHAPTER SEVEN

FUTURE AUDITS

Public criticism of the accounting profession, heard
for some time, reached a crescendo in the aftermath
of the Enron bankruptcy. "Where were the auditors?" This
question has been much asked since Enron, with almost no
warning, sought bankruptcy protection a mere four weeks
after its announcement of the need to restate its financial
statements. The follow-up question: "How could this happen to a company that had received an unqualified auditor's opinion on its historical financial statements for so
many years?"

Enron is just one example of a recent spate of business
failures that occurred with virtually no prior public expres-
sion of concern over the reliability of the company's financial reporting on the part of the independent auditing firm.
Not surprisingly, the full spectrum of news media commen-
tators in the United States and around the world has had
much to say on this issue. Derisive jokes about corruption
and scandal have replaced harmless humor about bean coun-
ters. Those who have been hurt financially and personally
find none of this a laughing matter—nor does the auditing

profession. The public outcry has struck at the heart of its professional values: objectivity, independence, and integrity.

Some of the criticism is just and thoughtful; some is off the mark. The most fervent critics point to the flawed aspects of the current financial reporting and auditing system and contend that little substantive change has occurred in nearly 70 years. Their answer? "Silver bullet" solutions that amount to little more than piecemeal reforms to address symptoms instead of root causes. In a time of challenge, when public confidence in the system has been threatened, the participants in the Corporate Reporting Supply Chain should look beyond creating patches for today's problems. They should look for creative solutions to the fundamental issues.

This much is abundantly clear: independent auditing firms must address the questions raised about the quality and relevance of their work. They must do this quickly because public trust is fragile—easy to lose and hard to regain. While audit failure is not the root cause of business failure, a dramatic business failure with no warning from the auditor can shake the foundation of public trust on which the capital markets rely.

One of the central propositions of this book is that when investors have access to more reliable and more timely information about company performance—in large measure, the information that executives use to run their businesses—better investment decisions will be possible. Such an environment could considerably lessen the incentives to minimize disclosure of meaningful information or to obscure troublesome facts. If markets begin to reward companies that swiftly, fully, and accurately describe their performance, the pressure to play The Earnings Game—and for auditors to acquiesce in it—will also be relieved.

The possibility becomes real that the auditor's role will shift from reporting that financial statements materially adhere to exacting rules, to one of helping to assure that the financial statement presentation of corporate performance is complete, accurate, and understandable for investors and other stakeholders.

The Three-Tier Model of Corporate Transparency provides the information that is relevant to investors and other stakeholders for the decisions they must make. The reliability of this information is assured by subjecting it to an audit by an independent and objective third party.

That assurance begins at Tier One, which is the focus of what auditing firms do today. Because auditing firms assure the financial statements and occupy the final link in the Corporate Reporting Supply Chain (see Exhibit 7.1) before financial information is publicly reported, their role is crucial in building public trust. They bring independence and objectivity to their task. In the future, investors will benefit if assurance extends to Tiers Two and Three. This will require assurance on a broader and deeper set of information, more frequently provided, and on a more timely basis.

Exhibit 7.1
Independent Auditors in the
Corporate Reporting Supply Chain

No level of assurance, even of the highest quality, can replace investors' need for analysis of the information they receive. Poor-quality information that results from flawed or nonexistent assurance makes high-quality analysis nearly impossible, although assurance alone cannot guarantee the quality of analysis. A balance must be struck: Investors and other stakeholders deserve high-quality assurance, but they must also assume responsibility for doing or obtaining high-quality analysis.

THE EXPECTATIONS GAP

Under the traditional model of corporate reporting, controversies have continually erupted over what the auditor's role is and what it ought to be. Differences of opinion about the level of assurance that the auditor's report should convey could have been described as an *Expectations Gap*. For years, attempts have been made to educate the public about the role—carefully circumscribed by laws or local norms—that auditors actually play. These efforts appear to have met with little success. Yet, the promise of future audits is constrained by antiquated laws, rigid rules, punitive legal systems that chill innovation in corporate reporting—and by the auditing profession's reluctance to accept a broader charter that would entail wider responsibility, greater controversy, and more risk.

The specific criticisms of the accounting profession, and their intensity, vary from country to country. They are directed at both generally accepted accounting principles (GAAP) and generally accepted auditing standards (GAAS). For example, as discussed in some detail in Chapter 2, U.S. GAAP is often criticized as being too "rules-based." A common criticism of GAAS is that auditing firms do not go far enough to detect material errors in financial statements due to fraud. Another criticism is that auditing standards are not the same around the world, making comparability of audit opinions among countries more difficult. Only three years ago, the Far East financial crisis illustrated the importance of consistently high-quality and transparent accounting and auditing standards as an essential ingredient of market and financial stability.

THE AUDIT OPINION

The sample audit opinion in Exhibit 7.2 is in the format of a basic audit report for an engagement conducted in accordance with International Standards on Auditing. It conveys the carefully defined responsibility that auditors take today for the financial information prepared by management, approved by the board of directors, audited by the independent auditor, and reported publicly to investors and other stakeholders.

Auditors worldwide issue similar reports on prescribed financial statements, with minor variations to reflect local accounting, auditing, legal, and other regulatory requirements. For example, in Germany the report on listed companies also requires the auditor to conclude whether "on the whole, the group management report provides a suitable understanding of the group's position and suitably presents the risks of future development." In the United Kingdom the audit opinion on listed companies includes, "We also report to you if, in our opinion, the directors' report is not consistent with the financial statements, if the company has not kept proper accounting records, if we have not received all the information and explanations we require for our audit, or if information specified by law or the

Exhibit 7.2
Extract of Language from
Today's Financial Audit Opinion

Report of Independent Auditors
To the Board of Directors and Shareholders of ABC Corporation:

We have audited the accompanying balance sheet of the ABC Company and its subsidiaries (the 'Group') as of December 31, 200X, and the related consolidated statements of income, and cash flows for the year then ended. These financial statements are the responsibility of the Group's management. Our responsibility is to express an opinion on these financial statements based on our audit.

We conducted our audit in accordance with International Standards on Auditing. Those Standards require that we plan and perform the audit to obtain reasonable assurance about whether the financial statements are free of material misstatement. An audit includes examining, on a test basis, evidence supporting the amounts and disclosures in the financial statements. An audit also includes assessing the accounting principles used and significant estimates made by management, as well as evaluating the overall financial statement presentation. We believe that our audit provides a reasonable basis for our opinion.

In our opinion, the consolidated financial statements give a true and fair view of (or 'present fairly, in all materials respects,') the financial position of the Group as of December 31, 200X, and of the results of its operations and its cash flows for the year then ended in accordance with International Accounting Standards.

Source: Based on ISA 700

Listing Rules regarding directors' remuneration and transactions with the company is not disclosed."[1]

Ascribing more to these precise words than what they mean is the foundation of the Expectations Gap. Under the current system, auditors express an opinion on financial statements according to the exacting standards of the accounting profession, giving assurance in their report that the statements are "true and fair" or "fairly presented in all material respects." One could make the simple observation that the financial statements of today and the auditor's opinion on them lack the comprehensive information that would ensure accountability, and then blame the accounting profession for the shortcomings of the present system. Such simplification is not only unproductive, and some would argue even inaccurate, it also does little to make needed changes possible. What is needed is a concerted commitment by many parties—auditors, regulators, lawmakers, and the companies themselves—to make the future better.

Making the future better requires responding to the market's demand for audit opinions that say more about the information on the health of the business. Today, a great deal of this information is already reported by management, and for certain purposes is considered in the course of the audit, including such issues as management estimates, the possibility of fraud, risks, liquidity, and future scenarios. The audit opinion could be expanded to address this information, as well as how all the pieces fit together as a whole. Today, limitations on expressing audit judgments and procedures, based on the rules of how an audit opinion must be expressed, prevent this type of expansion of the audit opinion.

Rather than managing investors' expectations about the auditor's opinion, a better approach would be for the auditing profession, with the support of standard setters and market regulators, to take on a greater level of responsibility than they have today. While auditors' opinions can neither serve as investment recommendations nor prevent business failures, they *can* be more useful statements on the *information* that is relevant to assessing the health of a business.

In defining a greater level of responsibility, auditing firms must remember that the purpose of their opinion is to serve investors' and other stakeholders' interests, although the company pays the audit fee. Here the auditor must simultaneously maintain a good working relationship with company management, who prepares the information, while fulfilling its obligation to the board, which represents the shareholders' interests and must approve the reported information.

In the future of corporate reporting, the role of independent auditors will be refocused to give investors and other stakeholders assurance on a much broader range of information as embodied in the Three-Tier Model of Corporate

Exhibit 7.3
The Three-Tier Model of Corporate Transparency

Tier Three
Company-Specific
Information

Tier Two
Industry-Based Standards

Tier One
Global Generally Accepted Accounting Principles

Transparency (Exhibit 7.3). At all three tiers, management will prepare the information, the board will approve it, and an independent auditing firm will provide assurance on it. Providing assurance on a broader range of relevant information, in response to investors' expectations, will make the audit opinion itself more relevant.

TIER ONE: WHERE THE FUTURE OF ASSURANCE BEGINS

In the future, closing the Expectations Gap will begin with providing greater comfort on the Tier-One information reported in a company's financial statements. This will require broadening the definition of what is included in an audit opinion at Tier One. Although in some parts of the world assurance is already moving in this direction, accomplishing this goal will require a truly global set of generally accepted auditing standards (GAAS) to complement Global GAAP. In order for the auditor to give a more expansive opinion, some very legitimate concerns about legal liability, particularly in the United States, would also have to be addressed.

THE FUTURE AUDIT

A principles-based approach to accounting, as discussed in Chapter 2, is the best foundation for making financial reporting more relevant to investors and other stakeholders. The broader principles-based framework assigns responsibility to management to select the most appropriate accounting methods to reflect the economics of the transaction, not just those accounting methods dictated by narrow rules. Principles allow management scope to explain in appropriate detail how the principles have been applied and why. Principles also require that auditors exercise more judgment as well.

In a future world of Tier-One financial statements, management would prepare them with six objectives in mind:

1. *Completeness,* in a forthright and balanced manner, of the information reported in the financial statements, mindful of the information reported at Tiers Two and Three, to make the financial statements a better platform for analysis.

2. *Compliance* with the spirit of principles-based Global GAAP regarding management's selection and application of the accounting methods that report the substance of transactions and are most appropriate in the circumstances.

3. *Consistency* in the application of accounting principles between periods to make historical information more useful for extrapolating future results.

4. *Commentary* on risks and uncertainties, including significant estimates used by management and the quality of accounting and management controls.

5. *Clarity* of the company's reporting to stakeholders in terms of how all of the elements of the Three-Tier Model relate to each other.

6. *Communicating* in plain language and using reporting formats, such as XBRL, to make the financial statements as useful as possible.

The role of the auditing firm would be to work with management to help it accomplish these "Six C" objectives, since issuing an audit opinion would require that these objectives be met to some standard. Various levels of an audit opinion might be given in contrast to the "pass/fail" model used today. These "grades" could be for all of the Six Cs taken together, or even for each in turn. More expansive audit opinions would provide a greater level of assurance to stakeholders, while creating an incentive for companies to improve their corporate reporting practices.

GLOBAL GAAS

Realizing the broader intent of this future audit opinion will require development of a set of global generally accepted auditing standards (Global GAAS) to ensure that the necessary work has been done to make the audit opinion credible. Today the quality of auditing standards varies in different parts of the world. This variation must be eliminated, and all audits of Global GAAP statements be performed according to Global GAAS.

Chapter 2 discussed how the convergence of International Financial Reporting Standards (IFRS), U.S. GAAP, and other major GAAPs could lead to a truly global set of generally accepted accounting principles (Global GAAP). Taking the best of today's International Standards on Auditing (ISA) and combining them with the best of other auditing standards, such as U.K. GAAS and U.S. GAAS, could accomplish a similar convergence of auditing standards. To make this happen, the International Auditing and Assurance Standards Board (IAASB) (www.ifac.org/IAASB),[2] the group that establishes ISA, needs to work with leading national auditing standard setters.

This process has already begun, and several joint projects between the IAASB and national organizations are under way. But the efforts must go farther. The International

Standards on Auditing must be significantly improved to take into account the high degree of complexity of some of the world's largest corporations and the risks involved in managing and auditing them. This would require mechanisms for establishing and updating a set of global generally accepted auditing standards, much the same as will be needed to make Global GAAP a reality. Endorsement of ISA by market regulators, such as the European Commission (EC) and the Securities and Exchange Commission (SEC) in the United States, would also be very valuable toward encouraging all auditing firms to use them. Enforcing these auditing standards could be done on a country-by-country basis, using whatever mechanisms are currently in place to review the quality of the audits being performed.

BEYOND TIER-ONE ASSURANCE

The reliability of corporate reporting and the effort to close the Expectations Gap depend on more than enhanced Tier-One assurance. They also depend on independent assurance on information at Tiers Two and Three. Tier-Two and Tier-Three information is highly relevant to investors and stakeholders, but of questionable reliability since virtually no independent assurance is given on this information today. Furthermore, independent assurance also needs to expand to address the level of data quality and to provide more timely audits of more frequently reported information. As assurance expands, liability issues would need to be addressed in the same way they will need to be addressed for more expansive Tier-One audit opinions.

ASSURANCE AT TIER TWO AND TIER THREE

The quality of analysis in decision making is severely compromised when analysts and investors use information that is not reliable. That is why assurance plays such a critical role in establishing a credible analytic foundation for the allocation of capital in the global markets. Increasingly, the information used in analysis will be the information at Tier Two and Tier Three. Providing assurance on this information will also help to close the Expectations Gap.

Providing independent assurance on Tier-Two information would be similar, but not identical, to the audit of financial statements at Tier One. It would be similar because it would be based on whether the company had adhered to Tier-Two, principles-based standards—standards that would require information from both inside and outside of the company. The primary objectives for this assurance would be to communicate to all stakeholders that the information was prepared and reported in compliance with the prevailing industry-based standards, consistently applied, and reported with clarity and completeness to give a balanced picture of the company's performance.

Despite the similarity, a major difference would exist between a Tier-One and a Tier-Two audit. A Tier-One audit, like audits today, would take a "big picture" view of all the information combined into the financial statements as a whole. Here compliance with accounting standards as to particular balances is not enough. Completeness is necessary as well.

In the early stages of assurance at Tier Two, overall GAAP-like frameworks would be unlikely to exist for particular value driver categories such as human capital or customer care, let alone for Tier-Two information as a whole. While assurance could be provided on particular measures within any given category in terms of compliance, it would be less likely, at least initially, that assurance could be provided in terms of completeness. This could only be done once overarching frameworks were developed that included all of the components in a value driver category, similar to the goal of Global GAAP at Tier One.

Where the company-specific information at Tier Three is concerned, assurance would be qualitatively quite different because it would not be based on a well-defined set of external standards. Compliance with standards, therefore, would not be an objective of assurance at Tier Three. Recall that Tier-Three information includes statements about the company's strategy, how it is managing risk, its approach to corporate governance, compensation policies, performance measures calculated in a way unique to the company, and projections and plans. Consequently, the *form* of assurance provided would differ and might not resemble a current auditor's opinion at all. Clarity, completeness, and consistency would be the reporting principles of greatest significance to users of this information, and the focus of the audit's assessment.

While general standards or guidelines could be created for how Tier-Three information should be presented, the real issue would be whether the company *is actually doing* what it *says it is doing,* and in some cases how that stacks up against the performance of its peers. The provider of independent assurance on this point would need a great deal of business expertise and professional judgment, as well as the ability to compare and contrast information among companies.

DATA QUALITY

Data quality is a fundamental assumption for proper management decisions, yet it is not an assumption that can be made in many companies today. A PricewaterhouseCoopers study of data quality, completed in 2001, showed that only slightly more than one-third of companies were *very confident* in the quality of their internal operating data.[3] Management decisions based on information of poor quality are unlikely to be good ones. The same would be true of decisions made by investors and others outside of the company were they provided with this information.

In the future of corporate reporting, users will have individual gateways for obtaining information and insights into the company. They will also have built-in analysis and decision tools enabling them to view data from a wide range of internal and external sources. This new reporting environment will challenge both companies and their auditors in novel ways. If these data are to be properly used by investors and other stakeholders to support their own decision making, independent assurance will be required at the more granular "data element" level. This is particularly true in an Internet-enabled Corporate Reporting Supply Chain where data can be separated from the types of reports on which assurance is provided today. This includes information from sources outside the company, such as a trade association or government agency. It also includes information from other external sources, such as an analyst's report or even a news release that may or may not originate from the company itself.[4]

Assurance in instances such as these can be accomplished using XML Digital Signature, described in Chapter 6. The exact assurance methodologies are still under development, but the broad adoption of XML Digital Signature will enable all users to see easily whether a given piece of information has actually been assured or not.

CONTINUOUS AUDITING

The migration of corporate reporting onto the Internet will continue to increase the speed and frequency with which information can be reported, both internally and externally. A company that has embraced the spirit of transparency will be able to make information available to the market as frequently as it obtains the information. One possible benefit of reporting with such frequency would be to reduce the market's episodic focus on quarterly earnings. More frequent information would make playing The Earnings Game more difficult for everyone, and public trust would be strengthened.

Continuous reporting will create the need for real time continuous auditing. Assurance will be provided more frequently and, to be most useful, more quickly. How useful would the assurance be, after all, if the data or information had already been updated?

Continuous auditing would not be done merely by working longer hours at a faster pace to do an "after-the-fact" verification of the reliability of a constant stream of disparate information. Rather, it would be based on auditing the systems and processes that produce the information in the first place. The assurance would then be given on how the information is produced. Every user of this information would also know that assurance had been provided.

Continuous auditing serves both internal and external purposes. Internally, it checks for errors in systems, for example, by looking for anomalies and/or patterns within a large volume of continuously published data. Externally, many potential customers in addition to investors similarly want assurance on critical information. Other external users might include banks that want to monitor loan covenants; insurance companies that want to verify environmental, health, and safety compliance; vendors that want to monitor a company's liquidity; and customers that want to monitor backlogs and promised shipping dates. The range of information that can be continuously reported and assured is as vast as the information that companies and their stakeholders rely on to make their decisions.

THE RESPONSIBILITIES OF INVESTORS

No matter how broadly, deeply, frequently, and quickly assurance is provided on information, an audit opinion cannot be taken as a buy or sell recommendation for a company's stock. Getting information more quickly and more often would not mean that investors could ignore the other elements of their decision-making process.

Between getting assured information and making an investment decision, investors must do two things. First, they must perform a rigorous analysis, using the information at their disposal, or obtain analysis from another source. Second, investors must be clear about their own risk profile: how much upside are they looking for and how much downside are they willing to take?

THE ESSENCE OF ANALYSIS

The purpose of analysis is to develop an informed view of the company's future prospects, to test management's view against that of the investor, and to decide if the stock is likely to perform in the future in accordance with the investor's risk profile. This requires a thorough understanding of information reported at all three tiers, including a holistic view based on how the individual pieces of information are related to each other.

To this must be joined additional information from sources outside the company, for example, about prospects and trends in the industry. Finally, a similar analysis of the company's competitors must also be undertaken. This comparative analysis, combined with relative valuations of other companies, is the basis for investment decisions. Investors who do this analysis on their own must hold themselves accountable for its quality.

THE RELIABILITY OF ANALYSIS

When investors obtain analysis from others—such as sell-side research analysts—they should take responsibility for evaluating the reliability of the analysis they are using. Reliability of analysis is as important as reliability of information. This requires that those doing the analysis be truly independent and work in a culture of accountability that values high quality and objective research. Because third-party analysts play a crucial role in the Corporate Reporting Supply Chain (Exhibit 7.4), they must take responsibility for performing their role well.

To assess the reliability of analysis obtained from third parties, investors need answers to such questions as:

- What information did the analyst use, and how was it weighted in terms of relevance and reliability?
- How have stocks that the analyst recommended in the past actually performed?

Exhibit 7.4
Third-Party Analysts in the
Corporate Reporting Supply Chain

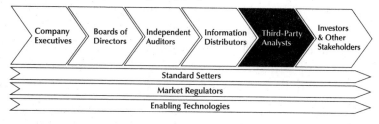

- How does the analyst fare when compared to peers by a credible and independent group, such as a professional association?

- What is the balance between the analyst's current buy and sell recommendations?

- Might something compromise an analyst's objectivity—a relationship with an investment bank, perhaps, or ownership of a company's stock—and how well are potential conflicts being managed?

- Does the analysis come with any form of assurance that it has been done objectively and independently?

An investor who makes decisions without answers to these questions is as careless as the investor who makes decisions without any analysis at all.

INVESTING MEANS TAKING RISKS

A crucial distinction needs to be drawn between the comfort investors gain from assured information and the level of risk of a specific investment. Stock prices can rise dramatically or decline precipitously even when the information in the public domain is reliable. Companies can go bankrupt even when assurance has been properly provided, and even under the reporting framework of the future with all of its breadth, depth, frequency, and speed. Even the best audit imaginable cannot eliminate business failure.

Investing will always mean taking risks. Those anticipating substantial gains should also be prepared for the possibility of substantial losses. This will not change in the future, even in a Three-Tier world of corporate reporting. Investors might have more assured information to analyze, but consideration of risk must still be part of their decision-making process. Those willing to give up some gain in order to reduce their risk of loss can choose less risky investments or manage their risk in various ways, such as through financial instruments.

No amount of market regulation can eliminate the possibility of loss. What market regulation *can* and *should* do, however, is to make sure that investors have a solid platform of reliable information for use in analysis, including information about the analysis itself. Building public trust should never be confused with denying investors' responsibility to make sound decisions based on high-quality analysis, clarity about the risks they assume, and their own risk management choices.

THE RIGHTS OF INVESTORS AND THE RESPONSIBILITIES OF ALL

The transparent future of corporate reporting and auditing advocated by this book is not inevitable. It will become a reality only if all participants in the Corporate Reporting Supply Chain seek to create a capital market grounded in a culture of accountability and recognize their individual responsibilities to stakeholders and others in the supply chain. They must work together across organizational, industry, and geographic boundaries to accomplish this goal.

As this book has insisted more than once, investors and other stakeholders must hold themselves accountable for the decisions they make. They will far more readily and willingly accept this responsibility when they know that the information on which their decisions are based is prepared, approved, and audited in a spirit of transparency by people of integrity.

Words alone cannot make this happen. The public must continue to exert pressure on every member of the Corporate Reporting Supply Chain, including the auditing firms, for them to act and to change. Without this pressure, the public will not get the information it needs and deserves.

However, pressure alone is not enough to ensure a sound future for corporate reporting. Leadership and vision are required. Individuals, companies, and associations of many kinds and in many sectors must rise to the challenge. PricewaterhouseCoopers pledges to offer leadership and support to this enormous effort. But no single participant can achieve all that must be done. Many informed and committed leaders are needed.

The publication of this book brings to public attention the results of a long and intensive process of reflection, debate, and global consultation within PricewaterhouseCoopers. It conveys the commitment of our organization to building public trust through leadership and by influencing each link in the Corporate Reporting Supply Chain. It is intended to stimulate a spirit of transparency that leads to actions by people of integrity. The goal is a shared culture of accountability. This is the future of corporate reporting. This is the foundation of public trust.

NOTES

1. Source of variations in audit report language: Germany, Institut der Wirtschaftsprufer; United Kingdom, Auditing Practices Board.

2. The International Auditing and Assurance Standards Board (IAASB) is a committee of the International Federation of Accountants (IFAC), the representative organization for more than 150 member professional accountancy bodies around the world. The IAASB was reconstituted in 2002 following a review of its membership, responsibilities, and process.

3. PricewaterhouseCoopers, *Global Data Management Survey 2001: The new economy is the data economy*, www.managingdata.com. Survey of 600 traditional and e-business companies in Australia, the United Kingdom, and the United States. Respondents reporting that they were *very confident* in the quality of their own management data totaled 37 percent among traditional companies and 54 percent among e-business companies.

4. Ibid. Only 15 percent of all respondents reported that they were *very confident* in the quality of data received from third parties in their e-business dealings.

EPILOGUE

◆

THREE FUTURES

Imagine three futures, each about 10 years out. In the first, disorder reigns in the capital markets because the impulse to reform the Corporate Reporting Supply Chain never moved past the "tipping point" at which good things could happen across a broad front. Doing nothing—so-called benign neglect—was the last best hope of those who saw the need for reform, but it has worked little magic. An inability to peer through the growing complexity of companies and markets has created new risks and costs for all market participants.

In the second future, a rigid and expensive bureaucracy enforces its will by ceaselessly adding new rules and regulations. The movement of capital hits endless barriers.

In the third future, a spirit of transparency is the guiding value. In that world, transparency cannot guarantee prosperity; there are still good times and bad. But public trust in the Corporate Reporting Supply Chain remains strong and investors have a better sense of how companies really create value.

Scenarios of the kind offered in the next paragraphs are necessarily painted in broad strokes. The three alternative futures may not be as isolated from each other as the scenarios imply—there may be patches of transparency in disorder, or bureaucratic institutions that lay a heavy hand on the workings of transparency. But the pure cases are nonetheless instructive by showing what *could be,* for good or ill.

SCENARIO 1: DISORDER

It is 10 years after Enron. All efforts to achieve significant and broad reform of corporate reporting have long since foundered. Good ideas and intentions were squandered in a political melee. For this, there was a high price to pay: The capital markets have fragmented into a vast free-for-all. One version of GAAP is pitched against another, and informed access to global capital has become prohibitively cumbersome and expensive, except for the very few. Companies publish more data than ever on their Web sites, more pages of numbers and text. But the meaning of what they publish has become more impenetrable than ever. The glossy photos in corporate annual reports are now three-dimensional with audio tracks, but management's words are one-dimensional at best and few bother to listen.

In this disordered future, corporate mistakes are often hidden until revealed by journalists. With so much shock and surprise baked into the system, shareholders routinely revolt, boards enjoy little trust, and markets lurch in all directions. Finding the link between value creation and reported results requires the services of an army of analysts, few of whom are completely above reproach. Only they can decode corporate information, but by the time they have issued their buy and sell recommendations, no one really knows where their information comes from and if it is assured or by whom.

The markets have become a global casino, fortunes won and lost on a single roll. The small investor comes into town by bus for the day, spends and likely loses a bit of "mad money," but no longer feels respected or even wanted. The worst losers form long lines at the courthouse to file suit against any company or audit firm still in business. Accounting and auditing have become commodities sold at only slightly higher than cost. Quality and independence are only as good as the buyer is willing to pay. Stakeholders? What are stakeholders?

SCENARIO 2: BUREAUCRACY

It is 10 years after Enron. The regulators are now firmly in charge. The fear of chaos in the capital markets and of flawed corporate reporting proved to be so great that the capital markets gradually became national and regional fortresses overseen by powerful agencies whose primary interest is making and enforcing rules. Closed borders prevent access to foreign capital, and investors have no option but to invest at home.

Only the regulators can set, interpret, and enforce standards. The Big Five have become the Big Two: the U.S. Department of Auditing (USDA) and its rival, the European Accountancy Tribunal (EAT) in Brussels. Asia, the Pacific Rim, and South America can only hope to come in from the cold—they have perforce built their own fortresses and despairingly await better times. The movement of capital, slow and cumbersome, is greeted with suspicion. Rather than accelerating the pace of innovation and new ideas, the markets hold everything back. Conservatism and myriad new rules result in a deceleration of growth.

The quality of assurance is only as high and delivered only as fast as can be expected from government work. Rather than moving toward daily closing of the corporate books, the pace has slowed. As a result, the only publicly reported news is old news. Meanwhile, analysts have gone underground, and black market research abounds. Investors can score if they find a connection and have cash to put on the table. The Earnings Game plays on, but now behind tightly closed doors. If you know the password, you might get to hear the whispers inside. Governments require all companies to report in XBRL, because externally reported financials are the basis for taxes.

SCENARIO 3: TRANSPARENCY

It is 10 years after Enron. The future of corporate reporting is now firmly in place. After sharp debate up and down the Corporate Reporting Supply Chain, the Three-Tier Model of Corporate Transparency has become a reality. XBRL, universally adopted by all listed companies, has proven to greatly simplify the Corporate Reporting Supply Chain while disseminating much more useful information. Investors and all stakeholders have access to a wide variety of software packages for conveniently analyzing information reported in XBRL. Global GAAP has been crafted by some of the most brilliant minds in several professions and from many different countries. It is supported institutionally by a strong interpretative function that collaborates on a global basis. It is enforced by market regulators who have the authority to penalize wrongdoing in ways not easily forgotten.

Recognizing the benefits of Tier-Two reporting, industries have developed standards for reporting additional financial and nonfinancial information. At the Tier-Three level, companies are providing timely and complete information to shareholders and other stakeholders in a way that is easy to understand. Most of the information used by investors is subject to some level of assurance.

The independent auditing firms have both the appearance and the reality of practicing at the highest level of professional skill, ethics, and independence. Third-party analysis used by investors is prepared in conditions that are free of potential conflicts of interest. As a result, capital is being allocated more efficiently all over the world. As an added benefit, the cost of capital is more realistically priced, and the overall cost of capital has come down. Good transparent companies, no matter where headquartered, have access to capital, and society as a whole benefits from such robust markets.

Society as a whole is understood to mean the peoples of all continents. A feared competitor in the software industry is based in West Africa. One of its rivals in the Gulf is worried about being blind-sided by the West African firm's newest offering. Innovation flourishes wherever bright minds and the entrepreneurial spirit converge.

All of this is possible. This is transparency. The public trust depends on it.

INDEX